What You Should Know About

The U.S. Constitution

And The Men Who Wrote It

What You Should Know About

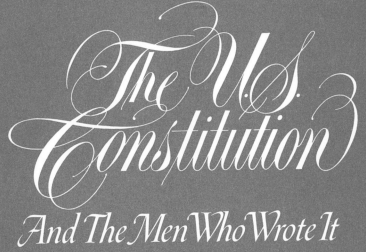

The U.S. Constitution

And The Men Who Wrote It

BY LeROY HAYMAN

CONSULTANTS

ALLAN NEVINS, LITT. D.
Professor Emeritus, Columbia University

VICTOR G. ROSENBLUM, PH. D.
Director, Program in Law and the Social Sciences,
Northwestern University

FOU — YORK

Portrait sketches by Tom Beecham

Cover: George Washington presiding over the Constitutional Convention in Philadelphia as depicted in a
19th-century painting by Junius B. Stearns.

Published by The Four Winds Press, a division of Scholastic Magazines, Inc., New York, N.Y.

For Anita…

my executive, legislature, and judiciary

CONTENTS

PART 1

Legend on U.S. Supreme
Court building reflects
heritage of 1787.

EWING GALLOWAY

The Curtain Rises

That Sunday in May 1787 was gaudy with springtime colors. Philadelphians thronged the wide cobblestone streets of their town, the largest in the United States at that time. Church bells were chiming, flags were flying. Revolutionary War veterans were firing their old service muskets and cannon to salute their hero and former commander in chief, General George Washington. (See *Washington* biography, p. 12.)

The General arrived in Philadelphia wearing his old buff-and-blue uniform with three gold stars in his epaulets. In the fashion of the day he wore a powdered wig under his three-cornered hat.

Washington had led the colonies' armed forces during the long years (1775-1783) they had fought to free themselves of British rule. And although he had been a private citizen for the past four years, he still looked every inch the soldier. At fifty-five, Washington's stomach was flat and his shoulders wide. He sat erect and easy on his carriage seat. He seldom smiled, but his blue eyes danced beneath bushy brows.

The Philadelphia City Cavalry and others who had

9

been under his command had met him on the opposite side of the Schuylkill River. Together the old comrades-in-arms crossed on the ferry and entered the city. As his carriage rumbled across the cobblestones, Washington waved and acknowledged the crowd's cheers.

"Speech, General! Speech!" went up the cry again and again. But Washington did not stop his carriage to address the eager onlookers.

The General's mind was undoubtedly on the real business that brought him to Philadelphia. He had not left Mount Vernon, his broad plantation on the Potomac River in Virginia, to receive the ovation of a grateful public.

Only one call could take Washington away from Mount Vernon. The nation he had helped establish was in trouble; the Union in danger of falling apart. Virginia had appointed Washington as a delegate to a convention to revise the articles of government. As a man with a strong sense of duty, Washington could not refuse.

Robert Morris

Washington had intended to lodge at the Widow House's boarding establishment at Fifth and Market streets. But his friend Robert Morris persuaded him to stay at the elegant Morris dwelling on Market Street near Sixth. The three-story mansion had once been owned by William Penn's son Richard and had served during the Revolution as headquarters for the British military governors of Philadelphia.

Morris, who had earned the name of "financier of the Revolution," had worked closely with Washington during the war, and they had written to each other ever since. Now Morris was one of Pennsylvania's delegates to the convention. (See *Robert Morris* biography, p. 49.)

Washington settled his baggage in a fine guest room in the Morris mansion, a chamber complete with brick

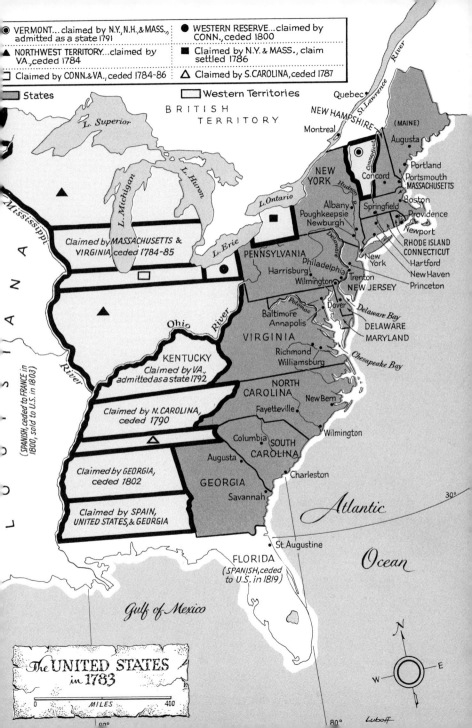

The UNITED STATES in 1783

GEORGE WASHINGTON

*"First in War,
First in Peace..."*

As chairman of the Constitutional Convention, George Washington stood on a bridge between two great careers. One career was completed. As commander in chief during the Revolution, Washington had led his country to independence. The other career was still to come. He was to be elected the first President of the United States in 1789.

Washington was born in 1732 at the Bridges Creek plantation in Virginia. When George was a boy, his father bought Mount Vernon. Later Washington owned it.

After tutoring at home and brief attendance at school, the sixteen-year-old youth became a surveyor. At eighteen he owned land; at twenty-one he was a major in the Virginia militia. From 1754 to 1758 he fought in the French and Indian War.

Washington married Martha Dandridge Custis, a young widow with two children, in 1759. The Washingtons had no other children. Patsy Custis died as a young child, and Jack Custis died during the Revolution. But Jack left four children, two of whom the Washingtons raised.

The plantation at Mount Vernon kept Washington busy before, between, and after his public careers. He died there December 14, 1799. In Henry Lee's words, he was "first in war, first in peace, and first in the hearts of his countrymen."

Mount Vernon, George Washington's plantation on the Potomac River in Virginia.

fireplace and four-poster bed. That same evening the General took leave of his host, walked over to the big house on Market near Fourth, and paid his respects to Benjamin Franklin. (See *Franklin* biography, p. 18.)

Benjamin Franklin

Franklin was the best-known man in Philadelphia and, next to Washington, the most famous citizen of the United States. Indeed, Franklin was even better known than Washington in the capitals of Europe. Through a long career, Franklin had become famous as scientist, publisher, diplomat, statesman, philosopher, and above all, a wit. Like Washington, he had concluded that the Union was in danger and that the national government must be strengthened. When Pennsylvania called upon him to serve as a delegate to a constitutional convention, he gathered up his waning strength to participate.

At eighty-one, Franklin was suffering from the infirmities of age, especially gout. As always, however, his talk sparkled. His wit, in speech and writing, usually had a sharp point. On the eve of the Revolution, for example, he had told the Continental Congress: "Gentlemen, we must all hang together; or, of a certainty, we will all hang separately."

That May evening there was no witness to the conversation between Washington and Franklin. But the General, serious and straightforward, and the old printer-statesman, quick-tongued and fanciful, no doubt recalled the glories and miseries of the past and made a careful survey of the problems that lay ahead.

James Madison

Washington was not the first Virginia delegate to arrive in Philadelphia. Already on hand for a week or more, and comfortably quartered at the Widow House's, was James Madison. Like Washington, Madison was the son of a wealthy man and owned a large estate in Virginia. Like Washington, Madison too had nourished a burning hope to see the Thirteen Colonies become a free nation, to see it grow and prosper.

Unlike Washington, however, Madison was not a man of physical action. He preferred to express himself in writing rather than on his feet. He was a thinker rather than a doer. At the meeting that was soon to start, however, thinkers as well as doers were needed. The business that lay before the convention would require the best brains that the country could muster.

Madison was later to go on to higher posts in his country's service, completing his life's work as President of the United States (1809-1817). But history remembers him best for this summer's work, during which he earned the immortal title of "father of the Constitution." For Madison, as we shall see, was to be the real mover and shaker among the delegates gathering in Philadelphia. More than any other, he was responsible for seeing that a constitution actually emerged from the meeting in Philadelphia that summer. (See *Madison* biography, p. 37.)

Many others were to have a hand in shaping the Constitution, and they were an impressive group. They were young for so important an undertaking (the average age was 44), well-educated (over half were college graduates), and prosperous enough to give their time and talent to their country. More important, they were dedicated, skilled in the art of government, and well aware of the importance of the job at hand.

The job required an impressive group. For the nation was indeed in trouble. It would take courage, intelligence, and foresight to re-establish it on a firmer foundation. The work these men were embarking on would affect the history of the United States and the entire world.

Chapter

1

Why a Convention

D elegates from eleven of the thirteen states gathered in Philadelphia for the start of the convention. New Hampshire's representatives came later, and Rhode Island never sent any at all.

Many of these men had had a hand in such matters before. For the Constitutional Convention was only one of many meetings — but, as it turned out, the most important — in which Americans had sought effective ways to deal with one another and with their common problems. The states, however, had not sent these men to Philadelphia for the purpose of writing a new constitution — as actually happened. The delegates had been instructed to assemble to revise the Articles of Confederation.

What were these Articles of Confederation, and why did they need revision?

Early Attempts at Union

As far back as 1754, representatives of some of the colonies had gathered at Albany, New York, to plan for the defense of their western land claims against the French, who had taken possession of the Ohio Valley. Benjamin

BENJAMIN FRANKLIN

Philosopher and Wit

Printer, author, inventor, statesman, scientist — Franklin was all these things and more. He was a thinker who could cut to the heart of a problem in philosophy or politics and offer a wise and witty answer. His common-sense solutions helped the United States come into being.

Born in Boston in 1706, Ben was the fifteenth of seventeen children. At ten he went to work in his father's candle-making shop. At twelve he was apprenticed to his brother James, a printer. At seventeen he struck out on his own.

Before long, Franklin was in business as a printer-publisher in Philadelphia. He organized Philadelphia's first volunteer fire department and America's first hospital. He invented the Franklin stove, investigated lightning as a form of electricity, and improved the postal system.

In 1766 he went to England to argue against the Stamp Act and stayed ten years. He returned — only to be sent to France to persuade that country to recognize the United States and help it in the fight against Britain.

Franklin came home to Philadelphia in 1785 and he was named President of the Pennsylvania Executive Council. In 1787 he rendered his last great service to the country as delegate to the Constitutional Convention. He died in 1790 at the age of eighty-four.

Franklin, sent to represent Pennsylvania, offered a Plan of Union under a federal government. The Albany Congress accepted this so-called "Albany Plan," but all the colonial assemblies rejected it as too radical. They were unwilling to give up any power to a central government.

Through the years the colonial assemblies had gradually won the power to levy taxes, appropriate money, and govern themselves with a minimum of interference from Britain. In 1763, however, Britain decided to tighten its control. The French and Indian War (1754-1763) had left Britain with huge debts, and taxpayers in England were already heavily burdened. To raise revenue, Britain imposed a stamp tax on the colonies. The tax was imposed on all legal documents, newspapers, pamphlets, dice, and playing cards.

The protest from the colonists was loud and immediate. In Virginia, the House of Burgesses debated, and then printed and circulated, the Virginia Resolves in which they denounced the stamp tax as taxation without representation. In Massachusetts, James Otis proposed an intercolonial congress to plan action against the tax. The meeting, called the Stamp Act Congress, took place in New York in October 1765. Nine colonies sent representatives.

In this early American cartoon Benjamin Franklin urged the colonies to "join or die." It was printed in the *Pennsylvania Gazette* in 1754.

JOIN, or DIE.

The Stamp Act, passed by Britain's Parliament, angered colonists because it imposed "taxation without representation."

Stamp Act Congress

Delegates to the Stamp Act Congress passed fourteen resolutions in which they declared that colonists were entitled to all the rights and privileges of British subjects. Taxation without representation, they said, was a violation of these rights. And they sent petitions to the British king and both houses of Parliament demanding the repeal of the Stamp Act.

Britain did repeal the Stamp Act, but it replaced it with import duties on many items including tea. The colonists tried to evade this tax by smuggling. But then the British Parliament worked out an arrangement with the East India Company whereby the company could bring tea from India to England without paying any duty there and then transship it directly to agents in America. The effect was to lower the price of the East India Company's tea in America. Despite the tax, the East India Company could now undersell not only other legitimate importers, but also smugglers. This was too much for some Bostonians.

When ships carrying British East India Company tea tried to enter Boston Harbor, Boston patriots, disguised as Indians, boarded them and dumped the tea overboard.

The "Boston Tea Party" (as it became known) angered the British Parliament. In retaliation it passed a series of laws which colonists called the Intolerable Acts. Under one of these acts the port of Boston was blockaded. Another had the effect of depriving Massachusetts of self-government. Throughout the colonies, patriots reacted with anger toward the British and sympathy for Boston.

Meanwhile, patriots in many of the colonies had been forming committees of correspondence. The purpose of these committees was to keep the patriots in the colonies informed of one another's activities and to provide an organization for resistance to any British injustices.

First Continental Congress

After Britain had passed the Intolerable Acts, Virginia's committee of correspondence called for a meeting of representatives of all the colonies — a continental congress. The congress was to frame measures, binding on all the colonies, which would force Britain to repeal the Intolerable Acts. All the other committees of correspondence agreed to the meeting and delegates were chosen by the committees themselves, by the assemblies, or by revolutionary conventions.

Delegates from twelve of the Thirteen Colonies met in Philadelphia in 1774. They passed a colonial bill of rights, which said that the Americans were entitled to "life, liberty, and property," and "all the rights, liberties, and immunities of free and natural-born subjects within the realm of England." They announced that they wanted to govern themselves, completely free of the British Parliament, subject only to the king's veto. They would con-

cede to Parliament a certain control over foreign trade —
but that was all. Yet most of the delegates considered
themselves loyal subjects of the king and — at this time
— rejected the notion of independence. Before adjourn-
ing, the delegates resolved to meet again the following
May.

By the time the Second Continental Congress met in
May 1775, the first shots of the Revolution had been fired
at Lexington and Concord. At first the revolutionary
fighters considered themselves "within the realm of England," but soon the idea of complete independence began
to catch hold. Step by step, America asserted its freedom.
With the Declaration of Independence, proclaimed July 4,
1776, all ties with Britain were broken. The former colonies — now thirteen states — were alone, outside the
"realm of England."

A bellman "rings in"
the Declaration of
Independence in 1776.
It marked the colonies'
determination to
free themselves of
British rule.

The State Constitutions

Even before the Declaration of Independence was published, the states began drafting their own constitutions. Between 1776 and 1780 all states except Connecticut and Rhode Island did so. These two retained their original colonial charters, which served as state constitutions for many decades. In fact, the new state constitutions themselves were based in large part on the old colonial charters. These state constitutions, in turn, served as models for the U.S. Constitution.

Each of the state constitutions contained a bill of rights, and all except Pennsylvania's provided for a two-house legislature. Each state constitution set up a system of law courts, and the top state courts gradually assumed the power of deciding whether or not a law passed by the state legislature was in accord with the state constitution. This doctrine of *judicial review* was adopted by the federal courts after the U.S. Constitution was accepted.

The Articles of Confederation

A constitution for each state was important. But with all the states involved in a common war against Britain, it was essential to have some sort of written working agreement under which they could operate as a unified nation. The Continental Congress appointed a committee to draft such an agreement, and on July 12, 1776, the committee submitted its draft. Congress debated the provisions of this new document on and off for about a year. Compromises were made, conflicts were resolved, and in July 1777, Congress offered the Articles of Confederation to the states for ratification.

The Articles provided for a loose alliance of the states. National power was to be vested in a unicameral (one-house) Congress in which each state was to have one vote. There was no provision for a separate judiciary or executive branch. Congress was to name one of its members as presiding officer, and he was to carry the title of president.

Congress was to have the power to make war and peace, to send and receive ambassadors, to enter into treaties and alliances, to coin money, to regulate Indian affairs, and to establish a post office. To finance its operations, Congress was to assess each state according to the value of land held by private owners in the state. It would then be up to the states to tax their own citizens in order to pay the assessment.

Within two years twelve states had ratified the Articles of Confederation, but Maryland held back. Before it put its stamp of approval on the Articles, Maryland insisted that all the states which claimed land west of the Alleghenies turn over those claims to Congress. While waiting for Maryland to ratify the Articles, the Continental Congress itself asked the states to yield their claims. Finally Virginia ceded its territory. Convinced that the other would follow suit, Maryland ratified the Articles, and on March 1, 1781, the Articles of Confederation went into effect.

Why the Articles Failed

While the war was on, a burning desire for freedom held the states together. They wanted victory, so they willingly cooperated with one another to make the Articles of Confederation work. But when the war ended, the United States began losing its "unitedness." Instead of cooperating with one another in the national government, the states fell to bickering.

Why didn't the Articles continue to hold the states together once the war was won? For one thing the states were tired, too tired to maintain the links that had bound them during the war. For another, the states had fought hard to win independence from Britain. They did not want to lose that independence again to a central government. Then too, there were weaknesses in the Articles, weaknesses which made it difficult for the national government to operate effectively.

1. *States first.* The biggest flaw in the Articles of Confederation was that each state could still put its own interests ahead of the nation. The Articles set up what was to all appearances a united country and then said: "Each state retains its sovereignty, freedom, and independence, and every power, jurisdiction, and right, which is not expressly delegated to the United States, in Congress assembled."

In other words, the national government could do only what the Articles said specifically it could do. The individual states had power to do everything else. More important, Congress could not compel the states to carry out its decisions. It had to rely on voluntary cooperation. The states were supposed to be linked in a "firm league of friendship" which was to be "perpetual." But with each state asserting its own rights under the Articles, the chances for real cooperation seemed slim indeed.

2. *Weak Congress.* Unlike our present U.S. Senate and House of Representatives, Congress under the Articles had only one chamber. In the Congress each state had one vote, whether it sent the minimum two delegates or the maximum seven. Each state chose its own delegates according to its own rules, paid them out of its own treasury, called them home and sent others whenever it wanted to.

"Yes" votes from nine of the thirteen states were needed to pass bills before Congress. That meant that five small states could join forces and frustrate the will of the majority of the states and of the people. An amendment to the Articles of Confederation had to be first passed by

Congress, then by the legislatures of all thirteen states. If one state failed to ratify an amendment, the will of the other twelve was frustrated.

3. *No power to tax.* Financial support of the central government under the Articles of Confederation was extremely shaky. Congress calculated the value of land held by private owners in each state. On the basis of this land evaluation, Congress then told each state how much it was expected to pay into the national treasury for general defense and welfare. It was up to each state to tax its own citizens in order to pay its share of national government support.

Congress never knew how much money it could actually expect from the states. It could not go over the heads of the state officials to tax the people directly and it could not force a state to pay its tax bill. Since there was no penalty for tardy tax payments, the states were often laggard in meeting their obligations.

4. *No real power to make foreign treaties and regulate trade.* Relations with foreign countries were supposedly in the hands of Congress, and only Congress had the power to make treaties. But after Congress had made a treaty of commerce with a foreign country, each state could — and many did — impose import and export duties just as it pleased. Thus Congress had no power to set up uniform trade regulations with another country.

5. *No national courts.* Congress had the power to set up temporary courts to hear disputes between two states, if one of the disputing states were to ask Congress to do so. Congress could also set up courts to hear cases of piracy and other crimes on the high seas and certain other sea disputes. There the judicial power of the central government ended. Each state had its own courts for all other kinds of criminal and civil cases.

Congress was not much more than a debating society

without power to compel the individual states to carry out its decisions. Yet during the Revolutionary War the Articles of Confederation worked — after a fashion. Why didn't the Articles continue to work after the war?

Wilson Criticizes the Articles

James Wilson, one of Pennsylvania's delegates to the convention, answered this challenging question in the fall of 1787. (See *Wilson* biography, p. 101.)

Wilson was pleading for Pennsylvania's ratification of the new United States Constitution that had been forged the summer before. He damned the Articles of Confederation in these words: "When we baffled all the menaces of foreign power, we neglected to establish among our-

The First Continental Congress, forerunner of the U.S. Congress under the Articles of Confederation, met at Carpenters' Hall near the State House in Philadelphia.

selves a government that would insure domestic vigor and stability. What was the consequence? The commencement of peace was the commencement of every disgrace and distress that could befall a people in a peaceful state. Devoid of national *power*, we could not prohibit the extravagance of our importations, nor could we derive a revenue from their excess. Devoid of national *importance*, we could not procure for our exports a tolerable sale at foreign markets. Devoid of national *credit*, we saw our public securities melt in the hands of the holders, like snow before the sun. Devoid of national *dignity*, we could not, in some instances, perform our treaties, on our part; and in other instances we could neither obtain or compel the performance of them on the part of others. Devoid of national *energy*, we could not carry into execution our own resolutions, decisions, or laws."

But long before Wilson indicted the Articles of Confederation for its many failures, there were others who were keenly aware of the weaknesses of the Articles. Among these early critics was young Alexander Hamilton. (See *Hamilton* biography, p. 40.)

Hamilton Challenges the Articles

As an army officer on General Washington's staff during the Revolution, Alexander Hamilton had complained that the Continental Congress could neither feed nor pay the troops. He had realized even before the Articles of Confederation went into effect that they would not solve the national government's financial problems. Why? Because Congress would not have power to compel the states to pay their assessments. Thus as early as 1780 he wanted to organize a constitutional convention with the power to "conclude finally upon . . . a solid coercive union."

After the Articles became effective in 1781, Hamilton

wrote a series of open letters to the newspaper *The New-York Packet* in which he kept hammering away at the need for a stronger central government. The new United States, he said, had begun life with only "vague and confined notions of the practical business of government." He said that until Congress was granted more power, the government was "unequal, either to a vigorous prosecution of the war, or to the preservation of the union in peace."

Hamilton's father-in-law was General Philip Schuyler of New York, a respected commander during the Revolution and later a member of the Continental Congress. At Hamilton's urging, Schuyler was able to prevail upon the New York state legislature to pass important resolutions. These resolutions asked that Congress recommend, and the states agree, in "assembling a general convention . . . especially authorized to revise and amend the Confederation, reserving the right to the respective [state] legislatures to ratify their determinations."

Both Schuyler and Hamilton realized, however, that a constitutional convention was some years away. The problems of a nation turning from war to peace demanded immediate answers. One such problem was an impending revolt in 1783 by U.S. army officers awaiting discharge.

Insurrection at Newburgh

These officers, assembled at Newburgh, New York, dispatched a series of complaints to Congress. They claimed that they had not been paid for months; their food and clothing allowances were long overdue; and Congress had not settled the matter of service pensions. It took all of General Washington's skill to soothe frayed nerves, calm hot tempers, and forestall the threatened mutiny. The officers finally agreed not to press their demands, and some even expressed their confidence in Congress.

The Newburgh flare-up was a warning Congress could not ignore. It had been told, in so many words, to find money to pay off the disbanding army.

Congress resorted to the only way it knew to raise money directly — it asked the states to pass an amendment to the Articles of Confederation. The amendment would permit a five per cent import duty, or tax, to pay the war-incurred debts. It also asked for special taxes on liquors, wines, tea, and sugar. These taxes were to be collected for the next twenty-five years and were to be used only to pay the war debts. Each state was to be given a yearly tax quota, ranging from $16,000 for Georgia, the smallest in population, to $256,000 for Virginia, largest in population. The annual total for the thirteen states was to be $1,500,000. In the future, these quotas would be changed to reflect changes in the populations of the states.

A tax based on population was a switch from the old method of taxes based on land values. But how many people, black and white, did each state have? Congress decided, following a heated debate, that after the next census was taken, the tax was to be based upon "the whole number of white and other free citizens and inhabitants, of every age, sex, and condition, including those bound to servitude for a term of years, *and three fifths of all other persons not comprehended to the foregoing descriptions* [our italics], except Indians not paying taxes in each state."

"Three-Fifths Compromise"

The italicized words were a roundabout way of acknowledging that a considerable number of people in the southern states were Negro slaves. The North wanted the slaves to be counted as persons, at least for tax purposes. The South wanted them to be classed simply as property, if persons only were to be taxed. The "three fifths" was a compromise that was to be later used several times in building the Constitution.

Congress sent the proposed amendment to the state legislatures. But the states lagged in their answers. Finally they got around to ratifying the amendment — all except New York. New York made so many demands for alterations and revisions that Congress finally gave up trying to push the amendment through. As we have seen, all the states had to vote "yes" if an amendment to the Articles of Confederation was to be adopted. Congress was forced to keep scratching for other ways to raise money to pay its war debts.

Another Insurrection

The Newburgh blast at Congress was not the only such rumpus raised by the armed forces. In June 1783, a rioting group of Pennsylvania enlisted men mutinied. Demanding their back pay, they stormed the State House in Philadelphia where the U.S. Congress was meeting.

Congress at once demanded protection against the rioters. But Pennsylvania's President John Dickinson would not call out the Philadelphia militia. He feared, no doubt, that the militia would side with, or at least sympathize with, the rioters. (See *Dickinson* biography, p. 32.)

Congress hurriedly recessed, and many of its members fled to Princeton, New Jersey, where they met the next week in Nassau Hall. Not many Congressmen attended the session and those who did were enraged. Congress had been disgraced, its prestige seemingly damaged beyond repair.

Hamilton Campaigns for Reforms

Alexander Hamilton considered the forced flight of Congress an insult to the whole country. Spurred by the

JOHN DICKINSON

Son of Two States

John Dickinson divided his loyalty between two states. He was a leader in both Pennsylvania and Delaware, filling high colonial and state offices alternately in each.

Dickinson was born in Maryland in 1732. After studying law in London, he settled in Philadelphia in 1757. He was elected to the Assembly of Lower Counties (later Delaware) in 1760, and became its Speaker. Two years later he served in the Pennsylvania legislature.

For a long time Dickinson opposed force as a solution to the conflict between Britain and its North American colonies. As Pennsylvania's delegate to the 1765 Stamp Act Congress he was against violent resistance to the law. In 1767 he began writing a series of unsigned articles for the *Pennsylvania Chronicle*. These letters maintained that reconciliation was still possible.

As a member of the Continental Congress, he voted against the Declaration of Independence. But he was one of the few Congressmen who volunteered to fight in the Revolution.

Dickinson served as President of both Delaware and Pennsylvania in the 1780's.

One of his last public duties was service as a Delaware delegate to the 1787 Constitutional Convention. He died in Wilmington, Delaware, in 1808.

riot and general unrest, he was even more determined to force a constitutional convention. In speeches and writings he repeated his charges. Congress had too little power. It was expected to be both legislature and executive, but there were no courts to back up Congress in either role. It could not regulate trade. It could not enforce treaties with other countries. It could not collect taxes. Nine of the thirteen states had to vote "yes" if a bill was to become law.

Feeling that it was useless to press for such a convention in Congress itself, Hamilton argued his point in newspaper articles, in letters to important men, and in talks to influential groups.

Slowly and indirectly, Hamilton's ideas were about to turn into action.

Forced to flee from mutinous troops in Philadelphia in 1783, Congress met at Nassau Hall (below) in Princeton, New Jersey.

Chapter

2

The Convention Date Is Set

Like Alexander Hamilton, James Madison was convinced that the national government would have to be strengthened if the nation were to survive. And like Hamilton, he worked tirelessly to promote constitutional reform. But their methods were different. Hamilton used a direct approach — letters to editors and men of influence, bills before Congress, and speeches before every group and assembly that would listen to him. Mild-mannered Madison believed in separating his bundle of firewood into individual sticks and breaking them one by one. If you cannot talk all thirteen states into working together right away, he reasoned, why not begin by bringing two or three states together for their common good.

The present trouble, Madison realized, was that each state jealously guarded its rights, privileges, and powers. No state was willing to share its prerogatives with another — even if such sharing would someday result in greater benefits for both states. Each state was acting like a separate little country — and just about as friendly as separate countries were toward one another in the 1780's.

Madison shrewdly surmised that a major weak spot in

any one state's armor of independence was its need to do business with another state. Already, in the 1780's, some farmers were raising more crops and livestock than their families could use and they were ready to sell their surplus. But the best markets were often in other states, and goods traveling across state lines were subject to duty.

Perhaps the states would give up some of their valued independence if it would mean getting rid of the duties and increasing the profits for their citizens.

Mount Vernon Conference

Navigation rights on the Potomac River were a case in point. In colonial times and under the Confederation, anyone who sent goods from Virginia across the river into Maryland had to pay a Maryland tax. Virginia likewise charged a duty on goods once they landed on Virginia soil. In 1784 Madison talked the Virginia legislature into inviting Maryland to a conference to discuss a reduction of the duties.

Representatives of the two states gathered at Mount Vernon in 1784. There, softened by Washington's hospitality and good cheer, the conferees canceled the trans-Potomac duties. Then they went ahead and canceled duties on Chesapeake Bay as well — duties they had not even planned to consider.

Foreign Trade

Heartened by this progress, Madison next tried to get the Virginia legislature to propose a resolution giving Congress the power to regulate all trade with foreign countries and among the states. Madison argued that European nations were reluctant to make trading agreements with the United States because they knew that the states could ignore any agreements Congress made. And the individual states were not strong enough to make

JAMES MADISON

"Father of the Constitution"

James Madison did not make a vivid first impression. But when acquaintances sensed the powerful mind behind the mild exterior, they respected and admired him.

Madison was born in 1751, the eldest son of a Virginia aristocrat. He was a bookish youth, and politics was a favorite subject. While still a boy, he foresaw the coming revolution. After attending the College of New Jersey (now Princeton), he joined the battle for political freedom.

In 1776 he helped write the Virginia state constitution. He fought for — and eventually won — a guarantee of religious freedom in the state's constitution. In 1780 he was elected to the Continental Congress.

Madison's effective leadership during the Constitutional Convention won him the title of "father of the Constitution."

Later, as a member of Congress, he helped set up the Departments of State, War, and Treasury. Thomas Jefferson named Madison Secretary of State in 1801. Together they doubled the area of the U.S. by buying the Louisiana Territory from France for $15,000,000.

Madison succeeded Jefferson as President in 1809. He retired from political life in 1817 and lived quietly at Montpelier, his estate in Virginia. He died in 1836.

favorable agreements themselves. As a result, almost all goods traveling between the United States and Europe were going in British ships, and Britain was reaping all the profits. Furthermore, Britain banned U.S. vessels from the British West Indies, thus preventing Americans from getting a share of the lucrative trade between the West Indies and North America. Madison thought that if Congress had the power to regulate all trade with foreign countries, the United States would be in a much better position to bargain for trade concessions.

Madison, however, temporarily overreached himself, and the resolution failed to pass. But he did not give up. Soon he persuaded the Virginia legislature to call a convention of states to "consider how far a uniform system in their [the states'] commercial relations may be necessary to their common interest and their permanent harmony." Madison's strategy was clear: a "uniform system" of national trade would demand central — that is, Congressional — control. Madison's long-range plan was also clear: giving Congress control of commerce among the states was a long step toward strengthening the whole system of national government.

Annapolis Convention

The convention was to be held at Annapolis, Maryland, on the first Monday in September 1786. Ten of the thirteen states promised to send delegations. Of the other three states: Georgia sent no reply; Connecticut made it a habit not to send delegates to *any* convention; and Maryland got the topsy-turvy notion that the convention had been called to cut Congress's power, and so refused to send representatives.

Madison arrived at Annapolis on the appointed day — only to begin a long wait. Of the delegates who were supposed to come, some never left their home states. Others started out but never reached Maryland. The final count was a dozen delegates: three each from Delaware, New Jersey, and Virginia, two from New York (Hamilton was one of them), and one from Pennsylvania.

Another Meeting Recommended

That so few showed up turned out to be an unexpected blessing. The delegates issued a report to the states that the problem of trade was much too important to be considered by so few states. They recommended "a future meeting," at which all the states would be represented. Delegates to this convention would meet not only to discuss trade relations but also for "such other purposes as the situation of public affairs may be found to require."

At first the delegates thought of recommending that ". . . the commissioners who may be appointed . . . should be authorized to deliberate on all . . . measures . . . necessary to cement the union of the states." The delegates then decided that this statement was a little too strong and revised it to say that commissioners to the meeting should have the power to consider "every other matter respecting the confederation." The report even set the place and time of the convention: "Philadelphia on the second Monday in May next."

Madison and Hamilton Collaborate

The report was signed by John Dickinson as chairman. But the ideas in the document came mainly from two men — Madison and Hamilton. Madison, cool and deliberate, was willing to arrive step by step at a workable, practical government. Hamilton, burning with the desire to see his adopted country strong and united, was all for leaping ahead.

These are believed to be Hamilton's words in the report: Problems "are . . . so serious as . . . to render

ALEXANDER HAMILTON
Political Firebrand

Alexander Hamilton added fire and passion to an already passionate age in American history. For most of his life, he was in the thick of battle — for the Constitution, for a strong national government, for a national bank.

Hamilton was born about 1757 in the West Indies. He came to New York at fifteen, joined the Revolution as an artillery captain, and later served on Washington's staff.

During the Constitutional Convention Hamilton often pressed, unsuccessfully, for extreme measures in the centralization of authority. But he did lead the convention away from several weak compromises.

In 1789 President Washington appointed Hamilton as the first Secretary of the Treasury. In that post Hamilton persuaded Congress to pass financial measures which, under his vigorous leadership, restored the credit of the United States.

Opposition to Hamilton's policies led to the formation of political parties. Hamilton led the Federalists who advocated a strong national government; Jefferson led the Democratic-Republicans, who stood for states' rights.

In the Presidential election of 1800 Jefferson and Burr tied — Congress had to choose. Hamilton swung the Federalists to Jefferson. Burr's anger grew, and in 1804 he challenged Hamilton to a duel. Hamilton was killed.

the situation of the United States . . . critical, calling for an exertion of the united virtue and wisdom of all the members of the Confederacy." Men at the convention must "devise such further provisions as shall appear to them necessary to render the constitution of the federal government adequate to the exigencies of the union." Formal in tone, the phrases were revolutionary in content.

Despite the differences in their temperaments, Madison and Hamilton worked closely together at the Annapolis meeting. It was a "meeting of minds" for them, and this fundamental agreement on policy was to produce important results at the Philadelphia convention the following year.

Shays' Rebellion

When Madison returned to Virginia, he found its legislature ready to consider revising the Articles of Confederation to give more power to the national government. Some legislators were even voicing the idea that the country was ready for a new constitution. What had brought about this change? One reason for it was the alarming news about Shays' Rebellion.

After the Revolution, poverty and debt were widespread in the states, especially in Massachusetts. To make matters worse, the Massachusetts legislature insisted upon a hard-money policy — levying high taxes to pay its debts and refusing to issue unsupported paper money to meet a currency shortage. Debt-ridden farmers in the western part of the state could not sell their produce for cash, and creditors would not accept the produce as payment. The courts were dealing harshly with debtors, seizing their land and jailing them.

In desperation, the farmers began a campaign to close down the courts and terrorize creditors. They were led by

Daniel Shays, who had been an American army captain during the Revolutionary War and was now a town official in Pelham, Massachusetts. When Shays and his men forced the state supreme court sitting at Springfield to adjourn, and boldly threatened to seize the confederation arsenal there, Massachusetts called out its militia. Still the insurrection grew. Massachusetts had to call on some of its wealthier citizens to contribute money to raise more troops.

Word of the rebellion in Massachusetts spread, and it frightened many people in other states. If Massachusetts could not suppress insurrection within its borders, could

NY PUBLIC LIBRARY

When Danel Shays and his band of impoverished farmers rebelled against the Massachusetts government in 1786, the national government proved too weak to act. In this engraving Shays and his followers are depicted taking possession of a courthouse to forestall heavy sentences for debtors.

any other state? Similar conditions existed in many states, and other rebellions against state governments might erupt anywhere. The whole nation, so newly established after a hard-fought revolution, could disintegrate.

Eventually, a greatly enlarged Massachusetts militia saved the confederation arsenal and put down the insurrection. Shays and other leaders were captured and sentenced to death. (All were later pardoned.) But by that time Daniel Shays, without meaning to, had convinced many states that a stronger national government was essential — if only to maintain peace and order. And when the delegates to the Annapolis meeting proposed a convention to revise or rewrite the Articles of Confederation to strengthen the national government, many state legislatures speedily approved.

Virginia Approves Convention

The Virginia legislature was among the first to approve the proposed convention. Soon afterwards Madison wrote George Washington, urging him to attend. The best possible delegates to the convention would be chosen, he said, "to give this subject a very solemn dress and all the weight that could be derived from a single state. . . ." The delegation, Madison told Washington, would be doubly dignified with "your name at the head of them."

On February 21, 1787, Congress put its stamp of approval on the convention. Congress could do nothing else, for without money or power it could see that the end was near. One by one the states named delegates — all except Rhode Island.

Rhode Island preferred to go its own way. It never did send representatives to the Constitutional Convention. And when the convention's work was done, Rhode Island was the last of the thirteen states to ratify the Constitution. (See p. 129.)

Chapter

3

Opening Days

The convention was scheduled to begin on the 14th of May 1787, at the State House in Philadelphia. The chamber that was to house the meeting was the same one in which the already historic Declaration of Independence had been signed eleven years before. The building was one day to become known as Independence Hall, and even now the chamber itself was sometimes given that name.

Travel was slow and uncertain in those days, and when the appointed day arrived, only two states were represented by a quorum (majority) of their delegates. One was Pennsylvania, the host state. The other state was Virginia.

Pennsylvania Delegates

Besides Franklin and Robert Morris, Pennsylvania was represented by James Wilson (whose scathing indictment of the Articles of the Confederation was noted earlier), Thomas Fitzsimons, and Gouverneur Morris. (See *Gouverneur Morris* biography, p. 111.)

For Virginia, George Wythe and John Blair were present in Philadephia, along with George Washington and James Madison.

No roll call was taken that first day, but all delegates then in Philadelphia probably attended the session — even Ben Franklin. Franklin's age and infirmities made it difficult for him to walk any distance and impossible for him to ride a horse. But he rode comfortably in a sedan chair carried on the shoulders of four convicts from the local prison.

With so few present, no business could be transacted. There was nothing to do but adjourn until a majority of states were represented.

Time for Talk

Over the days that followed, delegates from other states, singly and in groups, arrived in Philadelphia. Some came overland on horseback or part way in carriages. Some came by coastal vessel to the city's harbor. In the meantime, however, the long days of waiting gave the delegates in Philadelphia plenty of time for serious thought and for lively discussion about the task ahead of them.

At one point Washington revealed some of his ideas in a quiet but profound observation. His words were not set down at the time, but Gouverneur Morris recalled them twelve years later when he gave his funeral oration for Washington.

Answering those who advised caution and compromise, Washington said (according to Morris): "It is too probable that no plan we propose will be adopted. Perhaps another dreadful conflict is to be sustained. If to please the people we offer what we ourselves disapprove, how can we afterwards defend our work? Let us raise a standard to which the wise and honest can repair. The event is in the hand of God."

The Virginia Plan

By May 17 all seven delegates from Virginia had assembled in Philadelphia. While waiting for the convention to begin, the Virginians met each day for several hours "to form a proper correspondence of sentiments," as George Mason, one of the Virginia men, noted. (See *Mason* biography, p. 117.)

The Virginia delegates decided against trying to patch up the Articles of Confederation. Instead they proceeded to outline a new plan of government based upon their own state constitution. The plan, which came to be known as the Virginia Plan, proposed a national legislature, a national executive, and a national judiciary (system of law courts).

The national legislature would have two houses. Members of the lower house would be chosen by the people. Members of the upper house would be nominated by the state legislatures and approved by the lower house. Each state would have a certain number of votes in the legislature based either on its free population or on its "quota of contribution" (the assigned portion of taxes it paid to the national government).

The national executive (one or more persons) would be chosen by the legislature. Along with some members of the national judiciary, the executive would have the right to review laws passed by the national legislature and the state legislatures, and, in some cases, to *negative* (veto) them.

The national judiciary would be made up of a supreme court and lower courts. It would have jurisdiction over specific kinds of cases including any case in which "the national peace and harmony" was involved.

The Virginia Plan called for some provision for the admission of new states into the Union. It recommended that the national government have power to guarantee a republican form of government to each state. And it suggested that an amending process be established — one which did not require the consent of the national legislature.

Only a Beginning

The Virginians were shrewd enough to know that the first plan presented to the convention would provide the basis for discussion, and they were determined that their plan would be first. But they also knew that it was scarcely more than an outline, a beginning. They themselves wanted to be free to debate its provisions once it reached the floor of the convention.

Washington, the Virginians were virtually certain, would be named chairman of the convention. So they chose Edmund Randolph, Virginia's governor, to offer the Virginia Plan to the convention. He was, according to Madison, a man of "distinguished talents, and in the habit of public speaking." (See *Randolph* biography, p. 57.)

The Convention Opens

By Friday, May 25, a majority of the thirteen states had a quorum of their delegates in Philadelphia, and the convention opened without further delay. First in the order of business was the election of a president of the convention. Robert Morris, speaking for the absent Ben Franklin, nominated Washington. John Rutledge of South Carolina seconded the nomination. (See *Rutledge* biography, p. 107.)

Each state cast its vote, and Washington was approved unanimously. With his accustomed modesty, Washington accepted the appointment and reminded the delegates that he was without experience in such a post. None of his mistakes would be intentional, he assured the group,

ROBERT MORRIS

"Financier of the Revolution"

Napoleon's well-remembered dictum that an army marches on its stomach certainly applied to American forces during the Revolution. And the man who almost single-handedly raised the money to buy food, clothes, and munitions was Robert Morris, the "financier of the Revolution."

Robert Morris was born in England in 1734. At thirteen he joined his father, a tobacco exporter, in Maryland. Moving to Philadelphia, Morris went to work for a firm of shipping merchants. A full partner at twenty, Morris raised the firm to first rank — and made himself rich.

When Britain imposed a stamp tax on the American colonies in 1765, Morris sided with the colonists. Eleven years later, he signed the Declaration of Independence.

Congress chose Morris as Superintendent of Finance in 1781. He resigned three years later in despair over Congress' inability to make the states pay what they owed. But by then he had already financed the Battle of Yorktown which brought victory to the Americans.

After the Constitutional Convention, Morris served as U.S. Senator from Pennsylvania. Land speculations finally drove him into bankruptcy, and he was jailed from 1798 to 1801. Sick and dispirited, he died in 1806.

and he hoped they might be forgiven. Twelve years before, in the same room, he had been named commander in chief of America's army, and he had accepted the appointment in much the same spirit.

Major William Jackson of South Carolina was chosen secretary. A committee made up of Wythe of Virginia, Hamilton of New York, and Charles Pinckney of South Carolina was appointed to draw up rules of order for the convention's business. The convention then adjourned until the following Monday, May 28.

Rules of Procedure

Monday opened with a discussion of a draft of the proposed rules. Without much debate the delegates decided on their working procedure. Voting would be by states, with each state polling its delegates to decide what its vote would be. The business of the convention would proceed as long as seven or more states were represented, and a majority of those present could make decisions.

One major rule proposed would have permitted any delegate to call for the "yeas and nays" on any vote and have them recorded in the minutes. But the delegates foresaw that they would be changing their minds, perhaps more than once, as the discussion proceeded. They did not want to be hobbled by earlier decisions when new facts or points of view suggested a change in vote. So they rejected this proposed rule.

The convention did adopt another proposed rule — one which kept hidden the full details of its proceedings. The rule directed: "That no copy be taken of any entry on the journal during the sitting of the House without the leave of the House. That members only be permitted to inspect the journal. That nothing spoken in the House be printed, or otherwise published, or communicated without leave."

Thomas Jefferson, author of the Declaration of Independence and, later, third President of the United States, was in Paris as U.S. Minister to France when he learned of this rule. He wrote that he was "sorry they began their deliberations by so abominable a precedent as that of tying up the tongues of their members." (See *Jefferson* biography, p. 67.)

Madison, writing in 1830, about forty-three years after the convention, held a contrary opinion. He claimed that if the convention proceedings had been open, the Constitution would never have been created. Secrecy was vital, he said, "because opinions were so various and at first so crude that it was necessary they should be long debated before any uniform system of opinion could be formed. Meantime the minds of the members were changing, and much was to be gained by a yielding and accommodating spirit. Had the members committed themselves publicly at first, they would have afterwards supposed consistency required them to maintain their ground, whereas by secret discussion no man felt himself obliged to retain his opinions any longer than he was satisfied of their propriety and truth, and was open to the force of argument."

The delegates decided on secrecy because they wanted to receive credit for *what* they created, not *how* they created it.

Madison's Notes

The secretary's journal was finally published in 1819, but it contained only the sketchiest description of what happened during those fateful days. Fortunately, several of the delegates kept diaries, and these were published after 1821. But not until Madison's private notes were published in 1840 was the picture filled in. Although somewhat dry and formal, they proved to be a treasure house of details.

Madison apparently considered himself the unofficial convention recorder. Here, in his own words, is how he went about his job. "I chose a seat in front of the presiding member [Washington], with the other members on my right hand and left hand. In this favorable position for hearing all that passed I noted in terms legible and abbreviations and marks intelligible to myself what was read from the Chair or spoken by the members; and losing not a moment unnecessarily between the adjournment and reassembling of the convention I was enabled to write out my daily notes during the session or within a few finishing days after its close. . . . It happened also that I was not absent a single day, nor more than a casual fraction of an hour in any day, so that I could not have lost a single speech, unless a very short one."

The reader who applies a bit of imagination to Madison's notes can picture in his mind's eye the events of that long, hot summer in Philadelphia. He can see real flesh-and-blood men sweating beneath their powdered wigs. He can observe the clashes of opinion and the pauses for crucial votes, the thundering speeches and the swift retorts or casual remarks cutting the ground from under too-pompous orators. Imagination can turn the dusty record of the Constitutional Convention into an exciting real-life drama — a drama that brought into being our government, our freedoms, and our responsibilities.

Washington Admonishes Delegates

With secrecy the rule, the day-to-day proceedings of the convention seldom leaked out. Even State House neighbors knew nothing of what was going on inside the chamber. But on one occasion Washington did have to speak to the whole convention, and in the sternest terms, concerning a lapse of security. The delegates had been permitted to make copies of the Virginia Plan in their

While the nation waited, delegates to the Constitutional Convention met in long secret sessions at the Pennsylvania State House in Philadelphia (above) in the summer of 1787.

own handwriting. One day in June a delegate dropped his copy outside the meeting hall. It was returned to Washington, who held it until the end of the day.

Just before the meeting adjourned, according to Georgia delegate William Pierce, Washington rose and said gravely: "Gentlemen, I am sorry to find that some one member of this body has been so neglectful to the secrets of the convention as to drop in the State House a copy of their proceedings, which by accident was picked up and delivered to me this morning. I must entreat gentlemen to be more careful, lest our transactions get into the newspapers, and disturb the public repose by premature speculations. I know not whose paper it is, but there it is. [He threw it down on the table.] Let him who owns it take it." At the same time, continued Pierce, "Washington bowed, picked up his hat, and quitted the room with a dignity so severe that every person seemed alarmed."

53

Chapter

4

The Virginia Plan

With the rules adopted, the real business of the convention began. Governor Edmund Randolph of Virginia took the floor to present the Virginia Plan. Randolph began with a critique of the Articles of Confederation — how that document had failed to provide for an adequate government. Here are some of his arguments:

1. A proper government must be able to defend the country against foreign invasion. Under the Articles of Confederation, Congress could not do so. For one thing, Congress could not prevent the states from dealing separately with foreign countries, and for another, it did not have the power to muster an army or to raise the money to support it if war were declared.

2. A proper government must be able to stop quarrels among the states and revolts within them. Under the Articles, Congress did not have the power to do either.

3. A proper government must be able to provide for the welfare of the whole nation in areas where the states do not have jurisdiction. It should be able to control commerce among the states, for example, and to control navigation on rivers, lakes, and coastal waters from one

state to another. Under the Articles, Congress had no authority for any of this.

4. A proper government must be able to enforce its laws and protect its powers. Under the Articles of Confederation, the states could and did often ignore the central government and usurp its powers.

Randolph Offers Plan

Then Randolph read through the Virginia Plan (see p. 47). He explained various parts of the plan, but discussion was postponed until the next day. Before the meeting adjourned, however, Alexander Hamilton posed a basic and searching question. The first thing that ought to be decided, he said, was "whether the United States were susceptible of one government, or required a separate existence connected only by leagues offensive and defensive and treaties of commerce."

In other words, was the United States to go on as a group of states loosely linked by agreements, or was it to become one nation with one government?

Next day the convention turned itself into a "committee of the whole." This is a procedure by which the whole group still meets, but the formal rules are suspended until the committee of the whole turns itself back into a convention or congress. Sitting as a committee, the delegates could discuss the various resolutions of the Virginia Plan informally and take unofficial votes to gauge opinion.

Almost immediately the committee of the whole came to grips with Alexander Hamilton's question of the day before. Randolph introduced a resolution (as a substitute for some vague wording at the beginning of the Virginia Plan) which read: "Resolved that a national government ought to be established consisting of a supreme legislative, judiciary, and executive."

This was a bold departure from the Articles of Confed-

EDMUND RANDOLPH

He Changed His Mind

Born in 1753, Edmund Randolph was thirty-four when he served as delegate to the Constitutional Convention. His father had moved to England when the Revolution started. But young Edmund had already played an active part in founding the United States.

Randolph helped write the Virginia constitution and became the state's first Attorney General. He was a member of the Continental Congress, a delegate to the Annapolis Convention of 1786, and Governor of Virginia.

Randolph refused to sign the U.S. Constitution — even though it was based on the Virginia Plan he himself had introduced. He had wanted a three-man executive instead of a single president. He had hoped also that a second constitutional convention would be called to consider the work of the first one. But later Randolph changed his mind and urged Virginia's ratification.

Washington named Randolph U.S. Attorney General. Then, when Thomas Jefferson resigned as Secretary of State, Randolph took that post. But he resigned when he was suspected — unjustly — of taking a bribe from France.

Returning to private law practice, Randolph made a new name for himself. He defended Aaron Burr against a charge of treason — successfully. Randolph died in 1813.

eration. For a moment the delegates sat in stunned silence. Then the questions started. Randolph and Mason of Virginia answered them skillfully. With very little debate, the resolution was put to a vote. Connecticut voted "no." The New York delegation divided so its vote could not be counted. New Jersey, lacking a quorum that day, did not vote. The remaining six states present — Massachusetts, Pennsylvania, Delaware, Virginia, North Carolina, and South Carolina — all approved.

The resolution had passed. The convention was hardly launched, and already it was sailing in unknown waters. The delegates had decided not merely to revise the Articles, but to construct a new national government.

One State, One Vote

The next resolution ran into trouble. This one held that "the equality of the suffrage [in Congress] established by the Articles of Confederation ought not to prevail in the national legislature, and that an equitable ratio of representation ought to be substituted." The "equality of suffrage" under the Articles simply meant that each state, large or small, had one vote in Congress. The resolution proposed that representation according to population or wealth be substituted for one vote for each state. Under this type of representation the more populous (and richer) states would have more representatives and votes in the legislature than smaller (and poorer) states.

Strong opposition to this resolution came from tiny Delaware. Its delegates had been instructed not to accept any change in the one-state, one-vote rule. As a small state, Delaware would lose much of its voting strength in Congress under any representation-by-population plan. If the resolution were adopted, the Delaware delegates said, they might leave. A vote on the resolution was postponed.

Next day the committee of the whole agreed that the

national legislature should have two branches, unlike the one-house Congress under the Articles of Confederation. The delegates had long been accustomed to the idea. They had already seen it in practice in the British Parliament and in most of the American state governments.

Election by the People

Some of the delegates objected to the next resolution, that "members of the first branch of the national legislature ought to be elected by the people of the several states." Delegates from New England took the lead in opposing this step. Connecticut's Roger Sherman said that the people should have "as little to do as may be about the government." He wanted the state legislature to elect members to this "first branch" of the national legislature. (See *Sherman* biography, p. 75.)

Elbridge Gerry of Massachusetts — where Shays' Rebellion had taken place the year before (see p. 41) — was also against giving the people power to elect their national legislators. (See *Gerry* biography, p. 89.)

On the other hand, George Mason of Virginia said: "We ought to attend the rights of every class of the people." And James Wilson argued: "No government could long subsist without the confidence of the people."

Finally a vote was taken. Six states voted to allow the people to choose members of the "first branch," and the resolution passed. But the question was not really settled. Like other highly sensitive issues, it was to be brought up again and again. Now, however, it was laid aside.

Congress versus the States

The next important resolution to be discussed gave the proposed new national legislature power to "negative all laws passed by the several states, contravening, in the opinion of the national legislature, the articles of union."

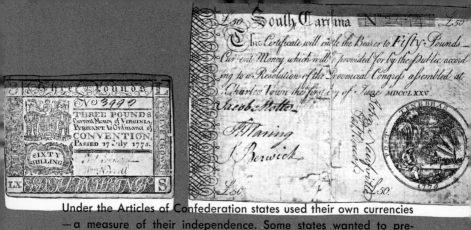

Under the Articles of Confederation states used their own currencies — a measure of their independence. Some states wanted to preserve their independence and power under the new constitution.

The delegates accepted Ben Franklin's added phrase: "or any treaties subsisting under the authority of the union."

What did this resolution mean? It meant that the national legislature could veto all *state* laws that conflicted with the national constitution. It could also veto all *state* laws that conflicted with the treaties made by the national government with foreign nations. It was a simple statement — but it proposed a significant change.

Under the Articles of Confederation — as the delegates well knew — the states frequently trespassed on territory set aside for the central government. States had borrowed money from foreign countries, for example, and maintained their own navies — both in violation of the Articles of Confederation. Congress could not stop them.

This resolution was an attempt to give the new national legislature the means to defend itself against such encroachment. And so anxious were the delegates to remedy this defect in the Articles that they passed it without a debate. Later they were to decide that a veto over state laws would give the national legislature too much power over the states. They were to come up with a different and more moderate solution.

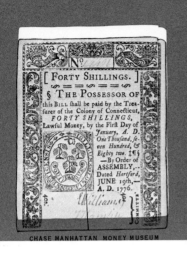

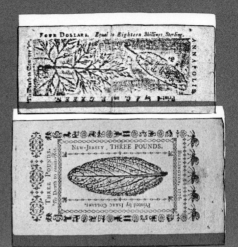

Checks and Balances

As June began, the committee of the whole laid aside the problem of separating the powers of state and national governments and took up the problem of separating the various powers of the national government.

At the beginning of the convention the committee had voted that the new national government should consist of a legislature, a judiciary, and an executive. Such a separation of governmental powers was not a new idea. Years before, the French philosopher Baron de Montesquieu (1689-1755) had written that a government could not deprive the people of political freedom if it were divided into three balanced branches — legislature, judiciary, and executive — each with a check upon the others.

Many of the delegates had read this book and others on the subject, and most of them supported the doctrine of separation of powers. This is what they had had in mind when they approved the idea of a national government with a separate legislature, judiciary, and executive. Now as the committee of the whole moved from the legislature to the executive and judiciary, and to the relationship between the three branches, these ideas were to influence its work more and more.

The Executive

In the sort of balanced national government the delegates had in mind, the executive would have to be much stronger than Americans were accustomed to, either in their state governments or in the central government under the Articles of Confederation. Yet memories of British rule were still fresh, and many feared that too strong an executive would soon become a monarch.

The framers of the Virginia Plan tried to find a middle ground. They proposed that "a national executive" be chosen by the national legislature to serve a limited term. They had specified that the executive should receive a salary, have power to execute national laws and "enjoy the executive rights vested in Congress," and share with the judiciary power to veto laws passed by the legislature.

Wilson of Pennsylvania opened the debate on the executive branch with a proposal that the executive be a single person (the Virginia Plan had made no mention of the number of persons making up the executive). According to Madison's notes, a lengthy pause followed this proposal. A single executive apparently sounded too much like a king, and the delegates were not sure the people would accept it. On the other hand, a single executive would be more efficient than a plural one. After some debate, the delegates decided to postpone the vote.

On the selection of the executive, Wilson again rose to speak. Why not let the people vote for electors, who would in turn vote for the executive, he suggested. This was the plan finally adopted, but the delegates were not ready for it yet. They voted against the plan and postponed a decision on selection.

Next they turned to compensation. Franklin opposed paying the executive. He explained why in a long speech (read by Wilson): "Have we not seen the great and most important of our offices, that of general of our armies, executed for eight years together without the smallest salary, by a patriot [Washington] whom I will not now offend by any other praise; and this through fatigues and distresses in common with the other brave men his military friends and companions, and the constant anxieties peculiar to his station? And shall we doubt finding three or four men in all the United States, with public spirit enough to bear sitting in peaceful council for perhaps an equal term, merely to preside over our civil concerns and see that our laws are duly executed? Sir, I have a better opinion of our country. I think we shall never be without a sufficient number of wise and good men to undertake and execute well and faithfully the office in question."

The delegates knew that Washington had accepted no pay for his war services. Some also knew that Franklin turned over his salary as Pennsylvania's President to several good causes. But the delegates took the realistic view that such men as Washington and Franklin were uncommon, even rare. Most thought the executive should receive a fair salary. Out of respect for Franklin, however, they did not take a vote.

Executive Veto

Should the executive have the power to veto acts of the legislature? This was the next question on the agenda. George Mason of Virginia fought vigorously against it. He felt that such power in the hands of the executive would pave the way toward a monarchy. Mason was backed by most of the older delegates. They feared a strong executive even more than they disliked the weak and impotent government under the Articles of Confederation. The younger delegates, however, were willing to take a chance on a strong executive. They counted on the people to keep the executive under control.

Washington sided with the younger delegates on this

issue. Later, he was to write: "There cannot, in my judgment, be the least danger that the President will by any practicable intrigue ever be able to continue himself one moment in office, much less perpetuate himself in it, but in the last stages of corrupted morals and political depravity. . . ."

On and on they went through the resolution on the executive, clause by clause. Despite the flood of opinions and the many postponements, most clauses eventually did come to a vote. After about a week of discussion, the delegates had approved most of the Virginia Plan resolution as it stood — and added a few clauses of their own. The executive, they decided, should be one person. He should be chosen by the national legislature for a term of seven years, and he should not be eligible for re-election. He should have power "to carry into execution the national laws." He and he alone should have power to veto laws passed by the national legislature, but two thirds of each branch of the national legislature should be able to override his veto. And he should be removable "on impeachment and conviction of malpractice or neglect of duty."

The Judiciary

Next on the agenda: the judiciary. With little debate the committee of the whole agreed that there should be "one supreme tribunal." But how would the judges be chosen? The Virginia Plan called for the national legislature to appoint them. Wilson of Pennsylvania preferred to have the executive do it. Rutledge of South Carolina backed the Virginia Plan. Franklin, feeling the discussion was becoming too serious, decided a funny story was in order.

In Scotland, said Franklin, the lawyers themselves chose the best lawyer available as judge, "in order to get rid of him and to share his practice among themselves."

The humorous suggestion cheered the delegates — but it did not help them make up their minds. They postponed the decision as to who would choose judges.

The Second Branch

Now the committee went back to a question raised before — should the national legislature be elected directly by the people or be chosen by the state legislatures? The question was one with far-reaching implications. If the state legislatures were to choose members of the national legislature, the state governments would be in a position to influence national matters. If, however, the people were to elect members of the national legislature, the state governments would be bypassed. The national government would be much stronger.

The delegates had already decided — tentatively — that members of the first branch should be chosen by the people. That vote was a victory for those who wanted a stronger central government. But what about the second branch? Who should choose its members?

The delegates were already calling the second branch the Senate, after the ancient Roman legislative body. This original Senate was at first made up of patricians — aristocrats — and some of the delegates had the same qualifications in mind as they discussed the selection of members of this second house.

Dickinson of Delaware, for example, wished the Senate to "consist of the most distinguished characters, distinguished for their rank in life and their weight of property, and bearing as strong a likeness to the British House of Lords as possible." The aristocratic character of the Senate would best be preserved, he thought, if the state legislatures chose the Senators.

Wilson of Pennsylvania thought that the people should choose the members of both branches. Otherwise, he said, "the two branches will rest on different foundations, and dissensions will naturally arise between them."

Mason of Virginia agreed with Dickinson. He argued that they had given the national legislature power to veto acts of the state legislatures which would protect the national government against the states. The states, he thought, ought to have some protection against the national government. The election of U.S. Senators by the state legislatures would give it to them.

Many delegates agreed with Mason, and the committee voted unanimously for election of Senators by state legislatures. Thus, according to the committee of the whole, the "first house" (later called the U.S. House of Representatives) was to be elected directly by the people. It was to be a "popular" house, in the literal meaning of the word "popular." The Senate, by being elected by the state legislatures, was to be one step removed from the people. It was to be the calmer, more reasonable, more reflective body. (Until the 17th Amendment was ratified in 1913, U.S. Senators were chosen by the state legislatures. Now voters in each state elect U.S. Senators directly.)

Cooling Legislation

A story — one that may be more legend than truth — illustrates the attitude of the delegates toward the intended purpose and role of the U.S. Senate. Thomas Jefferson (who, as we have seen, was in France during the Constitutional Convention) had breakfast with Washington after returning to the United States. Jefferson asked Washington why he had agreed to a second house in the legislature. Washington answered the question with another: "Why did you pour that coffee into your saucer?"

"To cool it," Jefferson replied.

"Even so," said Washington, "we pour legislation into the senatorial saucer to cool it."

THOMAS JEFFERSON

Voice of Independence

Thomas Jefferson wrote his own epitaph: "Here was buried Thomas Jefferson, author of the Declaration of American Independence, of the Statute of Virginia for religious freedom, and father of the University of Virginia." He considered these his most important accomplishments.

Jefferson maintained a lifelong love for Virginia. Here he was born, in 1743, and educated. Here he entered public life as a member of the Virginia legislature.

As a member of the Continental Congress in 1776, Jefferson wrote the colonies' document of defiance, the Declaration of Independence. Jefferson left the Continental Congress to serve in the Virginia House of Delegates where he proposed the bill that guaranteed religious freedom to the people of Virginia. That statute led to the same guarantee in the U.S. Constitution's Bill of Rights.

Jefferson was in France as U.S. Minister during the Constitutional Convention. When he returned home, Washington appointed him the first Secretary of State. In 1796 he was elected Vice-President and in 1800 President.

Jefferson spent his last years establishing the University of Virginia. He died July 4, 1826 — exactly 50 years after the publication of his Declaration of Independence.

Chapter

5

The Small States Speak Up

Up to this point, the committee of the whole had skirted the most controversial resolution in the Virginia Plan. On the surface this resolution had to do with the number of votes each state was to have in the legislature. But it went much deeper. It concerned the nature of the national government. Was it to be a government of and by sovereign states which in turn governed the people? Or was it to be a government of and by the people with the states playing a less important role?

Under the Articles of Confederation, each of the states retained its sovereignty. Each governed its own people. The states met in Congress as equals — each having one, and only one, vote — to try to deal with their common problems.

The Virginia Plan proposed a significant change — a change which would make the national legislature represent the people rather than the states. Instead of equal representation (one vote for each state), the Virginia Plan proposed proportional representation. Under this proportional representation each state would have a different number of votes in the legislature — the number to be based on its population or its wealth.

Not surprisingly, small states such as Delaware, New Jersey, and Connecticut, with small populations and little wealth, preferred the old one-state, one-vote rule. It enabled them to protect their interests in Congress on an equal footing with the larger states. They feared that if proportional representation were instituted in the national legislature, the large states would use their increased votes to promote their own interests and to defeat any measure that would benefit a small state.

New York

New York too wanted to retain equal representation in the legislature — and anything else that would keep the

Import duties on goods entering New York Harbor from as far away as China provided a rich source of revenue for the state.

state governments strong and sovereign. New Yorkers felt that their state had tremendous potential as a state. It was the fifth largest in population and had plenty of room for more settlers. It had untapped resources. And best of all, it had the port of New York. Several states imported their goods through the port of New York, paying New York's import duties and enriching its treasury. A strong national government, New Yorkers reasoned, would take over the state's power to collect duties on imports. New York wanted to keep the power and the money in its own hands.

Furthermore, machine politics were becoming entrenched in New York, and the state's politicians were against any change that would weaken their grip. Two of New York's delegates to the convention, Robert Yates and John Lansing, were under instructions from the state's political machine to support New York's interests first and always. The third delegate, Alexander Hamilton, was for the Virginia Plan or something even stronger, but he was consistently outvoted in the delegation by the other two.

The Nationalists

The small states and New York faced strong opposition in the convention. Many of the most articulate, informed, and influential delegates, like Hamilton, were opposed to any measure which permitted the states to retain their influence in the national government. These leaders believed that the strength of the states was the chief weakness of the national government under the Articles of Confederation. They wanted to build a strong and effective national government — one which could hold the Union together and foster peace and prosperity for all. These men put nation ahead of states. They were true nationalists and with good reason.

George Washington, for example, had commanded an army made up of soldiers from many states, and he had learned to consider himself first an American and only second a Virginian. As convention chairman Washington spoke little, but what he did say reflected his support for a strong national government.

Franklin too felt himself primarily a U.S. citizen. His years of representing the whole country in the capitals of Europe had taught him to put allegiance to the nation first and to state and city second. Franklin, addressing the assembly through James Wilson, also brought his influence to bear in favor of union, but with balance and a touch of merriment.

James Wilson

James Wilson, Franklin's chief aide among the Pennsylvania delegates, was born and reared in Scotland. His devotion was to the whole United States, his adopted country, not to one part of it. Blunt and honest, Wilson always spoke strongly for the need of a national government to lead the states.

Alexander Hamilton had left his West Indies birthplace at fifteen and eventually settled in New York. He considered himself an American rather than a New Yorker. As Washington's aide during the Revolution, he had seen how weak the Confederation was in supporting the war effort and how generally inadequate it was in peacetime. Although Hamilton had been almost silent since the convention started, the force of his brief statements demonstrated his conviction that central government must be strengthened.

Then there was Madison. A Virginian by birth and upbringing, James Madison had attended the College of New Jersey (later renamed Princeton University), thus widening his horizons. Service in the Virginia legislature and in Congress continued to expand his understanding of the whole country and its problems. Calm and slow-spoken, Madison influenced many delegates with the logic of his arguments.

These and other powerful figures at the convention did not want to do away with the states completely, but they did want to loosen the states' stranglehold over the national government. They wanted a true union of states headed by a national government. Such a national government would derive its power from the people, rather than from the states, and govern the people directly.

The Big States

Most of the nationalists were from big states and they were influential in their delegations. But there were other reasons why the big states supported representation by population. For one thing, they knew they would have a majority of the votes in the legislature under proportional representation and could look after their own interests. For another, they believed that since the bigger and wealthier states would be paying most of the expenses of the new government, they ought to have a larger voice than the smaller states in deciding how the money would be spent.

Nationalists versus Confederationists

As the convention wore on, it became more and more a struggle between the nationalists backed by the big states and the representatives of the small states or confederationists. The debate over proportional representation was the opening round in this struggle.

The first time this resolution had come up for discussion, early in the convention, the Delaware delegation had asserted that its instructions from home were to quit the convention if the one-state, one-vote arrangement were even questioned. Fearing that a vote or even a discussion of such a sensitive matter so early in the convention might break up the convention before it could accomplish anything, the committee of the whole quietly postponed the discussion. Sooner or later it had to be settled, however, and now the committee of the whole decided to tackle it.

William Paterson of New Jersey (for whom a city in that state was later named) opened the debate. The delegates, said Paterson, had been sent to the convention "for the sole and express purpose of revising the Articles of Confederation. We have no power to go beyond the federal scheme, and if we had, the people are not ripe for any other." Paterson went on to answer the argument that the big states should have more votes because they were going to have to pay more. There is no more reason for a rich state to have more votes than a poor one, said Paterson, than there is for a rich man to have more votes than a poor one. "New Jersey will never confederate on the plan before the committee" concluded Paterson. And, he added, he would rather submit to a monarch. (See *Paterson* biography, p. 79.)

Wilson was as outspoken as Paterson in his reply. If authority for government comes from the people, he said, then equal numbers of people ought to have equal representation. "Shall New Jersey have the same right or influence in the councils of the nation with Pennsylvania? I say no. It is unjust — I never will confederate on this plan. . . . If no state will part with any of its sovereignty, it is in vain to talk of a national government."

Sherman's Compromise

On that angry note the convention adjourned for the weekend. By Monday, tempers had cooled somewhat. Sherman of Connecticut offered a compromise. He sug-

ROGER SHERMAN
A Liberal Conservative

Roger Sherman is the only person who signed the Articles of Association of 1774, the Declaration of Independence, the Articles of Confederation, and the U.S. Constitution.

Sherman was born in Massachusetts in 1721. He received no formal education but read widely. As a young man, he moved to Connecticut, bought land, opened a general store, and took an active part in local affairs.

Studying law in his spare time, Sherman was admitted to the bar at thirty-two. He was a member of the Connecticut General Assembly for several terms and a judge of the Superior Court of Connecticut for 23 years.

A conservative, Sherman nevertheless fought against Parliament's control over the colonies. As a member of the Continental Congress he signed the Declaration of Independence, and helped draft the Articles of Confederation.

When Sherman arrived at the Constitutional Convention he believed that the Articles could be revised, but he soon saw the need for a new constitution. It was Sherman who suggested the so-called Connecticut Compromise which formed the basis for the Federal Compromise (see p. 89). In 1789 he was elected to the U.S. House of Representatives and in 1791 to the Senate. He died in 1793.

gested that representation in the first house be based on the number of free inhabitants in each state and that in the second house, the Senate, each state have a single vote.

Before the compromise could be put to a vote, Rutledge and Butler of South Carolina spoke up. South Carolina was relatively small in terms of free population, but it was rich in property, most of it in slaves. The South Carolina delegates favored proportional representation in the first branch, but they wanted it to be based on property, not free population.

Rufus King of Massachusetts, a large state, tried to head off another angry exchange by proposing that membership in the first branch be apportioned "according to some equitable ratio of representation." (See *King* biography, p. 125.)

Franklin Speaks

Franklin too tried to cool tempers. Wilson read Franklin's statement: "We are sent here to *consult*, not to *contend* with each other; and declarations of a fixed opinion . . . neither enlighten nor convince us." Franklin went on to give his support to representation based on population. "I do not at present see what advantage the greater states could propose to themselves by swallowing the smaller, and therefore do not apprehend they would attempt it," he added.

After Franklin's speech the delegates moved ahead into a rapid series of votes. King's proposal that there be "some equitable ratio of representation" in the first branch passed. Then Wilson of Pennsylvania moved that the ratio be worked out according to population and that population include "the whole number of white and other free citizens . . . and three fifths of all other persons not comprehended in the foregoing description [slaves]. . . ."

This was the old three-fifths compromise Congress had

included in its proposed revenue amendment in 1783 (see pp. 30, 31). It was included here to win the support of the southern states. By counting at least some of the slaves as people, the population of southern states would be increased, and so would their representation in the legislature. The strategy worked, and Wilson's proposal carried.

Nationalists Win

Next, Sherman of Connecticut jumped in again. With representation in the first branch based on population (including three fifths of the slaves), he proposed that each state have only one vote in the second branch. His proposal was defeated, six to five. Finally Wilson and Hamilton moved that the vote in the second branch be the same as in the first. Their proposal was put to a vote and it carried.

It was settled then. Representation in both houses would be based on population. The big states had won — temporarily. Would the small states now walk out and return home?

The next morning each delegation was in its place. The small states had not left. But neither had they given up. They were gathering strength for a counterattack.

Meanwhile the committee of the whole moved on to less controversial issues. The committee took up and quickly passed a resolution which stated that members of both branches of the legislature be paid from national funds rather than by the states — another victory for the nationalists.

Virtually the last of the resolutions generated by the Virginia Plan proposed that the final plan of government worked out by the convention be submitted to special assemblies in each state for ratification — not to the state legislatures. Once again the state governments were to be bypassed, and once again the nationalists carried the vote. The resolution passed.

Still acting as a committee of the whole, the delegates renumbered the Virginia Plan resolutions they had passed — a total of nineteen. Then the committee presented these nineteen resolutions to the convention.

New Jersey Plan

Before the convention, sitting as a convention, had a chance to take up the nineteen resolutions of the Virginia Plan, the small states rolled out their weapon for the counterattack. They had a new plan, they said, and they needed another day to formulate it. To give them time the convention adjourned for twenty-four hours.

On Friday, June 15, Paterson rose to present the New Jersey Plan. The new plan was essentially a revision of the Articles of Confederation. Here are some of the changes it suggested:

1. Congress would have some additional powers. It could levy import duties and regulate trade with foreign countries and among the states.

2. State contributions to the Confederation treasury would no longer be based on the value of land in each state, but on the number of free people and "three fifths of all others" (that now-familiar method of counting three fifths of the slaves as people).

3. The Confederation executive would be made up of more than one person and be chosen by Congress. A majority of state executives could remove the federal executive from office. This executive would serve only one term.

4. The Confederation supreme court would be appointed by the executive.

5. Laws passed by Congress and treaties made by it would be the supreme law in all the states.

WILLIAM PATERSON

New Jersey's Spokesman

New Jersey's William Paterson was born in 1745 in northern Ireland. When he was two, his parents came to America and eventually settled in New Jersey. His father started as a vendor of tinware, but he soon became a tinware manufacturer, merchant, and landowner. William Paterson was graduated from the College of New Jersey (now Princeton University) and went on to study law.

In the 1770's Paterson was a member of New Jersey's legislature and a delegate to the state constitutional convention. As a delegate to the federal convention, he was the leading spokesman for the New Jersey Plan (see p. 78). Some of its provisions were included in the Constitution. Pierce of Georgia characterized Paterson as "one of those . . . men whose powers break in upon you, and create wonder and astonishment."

Paterson signed the Constitution and worked for its ratification in New Jersey. In the years after the convention, he served as U.S. Senator from New Jersey, and Associate Justice of the U.S. Supreme Court. He was presiding justice at the treason trials of many who had participated in the Whiskey Rebellion of 1794. He sat on the Court until his death in 1806.

6. The executive could call out the armed forces of the "confederated states" against any rebellious state or "any body of men in any state."

Debate Over Plan

The convention turned itself back into a committee of the whole to weigh the New Jersey Plan alongside the Virginia Plan. Lansing of New York and Paterson of New Jersey took the floor in an eloquent defense of the New Jersey Plan. They claimed that the Virginia Plan was too radical, that the people would not accept it. The New Jersey Plan, they said, maintained a balance between the states and the central government — a balance which the Virginia Plan destroyed. The new plan revised the Articles of Confederation — the job the convention was called to do. The convention had no authority to propose the Virginia Plan, they argued. The Virginia Plan would be hard to operate. The cost of government would rise.

Wilson of Pennsylvania rose to answer their arguments, his words burred by his Scottish origin. The convention, Wilson insisted, was "authorized to conclude nothing, but to be at liberty to propose anything." He said the people were not at all so pro-state and anti-nation as the New Jersey Plan backers claimed. "Will a citizen of Delaware be degraded by becoming a citizen of the United States?" he asked rhetorically.

Randolph too defended the Virginia Plan. The future of the union is at stake, he asserted. The convention was authorized to find a means to preserve it. The Virginia Plan proposed to strengthen the national government by giving it real power over individuals rather than limited power over states. Under the New Jersey Plan, Randolph concluded, Congress would only be a "diplomatic body," and the Congressmen would be "always obsequious to the views of the states."

Hamilton Objects

At last Hamilton took the floor. It was the first time he had addressed the convention at any length. Hamilton said he was against the New Jersey Plan altogether, and even the Virginia Plan did not go far enough. He wanted a single executive chosen for life and a Senate, also chosen for life, that would serve the same role in the United States government as the House of Lords did at that time in Britain. The states would elect members of the popular branch of the legislature, but this branch would have less power than the Senate. The executive would have veto power over all laws, and the Senate would have the sole power to declare war.

Hamilton's ideas, so advanced and so radically different from what the delegates were considering, were received without comment. Madison, following Hamilton, returned to the discussion of the New Jersey Plan. He reminded the convention that if the smaller states kept pressing for the New Jersey Plan, the convention might well end with no plan at all to present to the people. Then the union of states would be dissolved into separate little countries, ready to be picked like ripe apples by aggressive European nations.

Vote Taken

Finally a vote to choose between the New Jersey and Virginia plans was taken. New York, New Jersey, and Delaware voted for the New Jersey Plan. Maryland, as on many previous votes, was divided. Connecticut voted with the other six states for the Virginia Plan. (New Hampshire delegates still had not arrived, and Rhode Island had refused to send delegates at all.)

Once again the nationalists had triumphed over the confederationists. Still the small states were unwilling to concede defeat.

Chapter

6

Compromises

When the convention returned to the revised Virginia Plan, the small states knew that they faced their last chance to win concessions. They also knew that they would be bargaining from a position of strength. The final plan would have to meet with their approval. If it did not, they would not sign it. And if they refused to sign it, what would be its chances for ratification?

Sitting as a convention, the delegates began to go over the revised plan proposal by proposal, making final decisions on each. The small states, fighting at every turn, were able to win some small but helpful changes. The words "national government" were struck out, for example, and replaced with "government of the United States."

A few minor issues were settled. The term of office for members of the first branch was changed from three to two years and from seven to six years for Senators. A third of the Senate was to be elected every two years.

Then the convention returned to the most controversial issue, the basis of representation in the two houses of the legislature. The committee of the whole had decided that representation in both houses of the legislature should be based on population including three fifths of the slaves. The small states, who wanted states rather than people represented, had fought that decision and lost. They tried to get around it with the New Jersey Plan and they lost again. This time they were determined to win. The big states were equally determined not to give in. The future of the Union hung in the balance. This was the showdown.

People versus State

The battle began with Martin of Maryland, who rambled on for two days in favor of an equal number of representatives for all states in both houses. The purpose of the central government, he argued, was to preserve the state governments, not to govern the people. The people had delegated their power to the state governments, and only the state governments could speak for them. The states were equal. They could not give up their equality to make way for proportional representation. Furthermore, proportional representation would mean that the three largest states could join forces to defeat the ten smaller ones on every issue.

Madison carefully countered this last contention. Large counties within a state did not combine to defeat small counties, he said. Neither would large states form groups to gain advantage over small states. Instead, he suggested, states small and large might link up for their common good or to promote common interests. Two tobacco states, for example, might join forces to secure legislation that favored tobacco growing and marketing.

Hamilton Speaks

Then Hamilton took up the banner for strong central government. Will the men of Delaware be less free than the men of Pennsylvania because Pennsylvania has more delegates in the legislature? he asked. The United States must have a government strong enough to ensure "tranquillity and happiness at home" and to command respect abroad, he said. This is "the critical moment for forming such a government. . . . As yet, we retain the habit of union. We are weak and sensible of our weakness. Henceforth the motives will become feebler and the difficulties greater. It is a miracle that we are now here exercising our tranquil and free deliberations on the subject. It would be madness to trust future miracles."

A vote on the basis for choosing members of the first branch was finally taken. Four states voted against proportional representation; six states were for it; Maryland was again divided. Representation by population in the first branch had won.

The Senate

The debate then moved to representation in the Senate. Again, were the Senators to represent the states or the people? Ellsworth of Connecticut moved that each state have one vote in the Senate. No northern state except Massachusetts, he warned, would agree to any other arrangement. Wilson of Pennsylvania opposed the motion: "Can we forget for whom we are forming a government? Is it for *men*, or for the imaginary beings called *states*?"

Franklin proposed a compromise. He was for letting each state have one Senatorial vote on issues affecting state sovereignty — to protect the small states. On questions involving national spending, each state was to have a Senatorial vote based on its contribution to the national treasury — to protect the large states. Franklin's proposal was respectfully received but quickly discarded.

Gunning Bedford of Delaware launched angry accusations against those who opposed an equal number of Senators from each state, large or small. The larger states, he shouted, wanted to control the Senate by packing it with their Senators. "Their cry is, where is the danger? and they insist that although the powers of the general government will be increased, yet it will be for the good of the whole; and although the three great states form nearly a majority of the people in America, they will never hurt or injure the lesser states. *I do not, gentlemen, trust you . . .*"

Bedford continued with an even stronger accusation: "Will you crush the smaller states. . . ? Sooner than be ruined, *there are foreign powers who will take us by the hand.*" (See *Bedford* biography, p. 87.)

Rufus King of Massachusetts answered Bedford's threat with a savagely polite rejoinder. King regretted that "the honorable gentleman from Delaware . . . with a vehemence unprecedented in this House, had declared himself ready to turn his hopes from our common country, and court the protection of some foreign land."

Committee Takes Over

There was no immediate chance of reconciling the opposing points of view on representation in the legislature. Further debate on the floor of the convention would have been useless at such a moment. The only solution was to choose a committee to help resolve the whole dilemma of people versus states in the legislature. This the delegates quickly did. Named to the committee were Gerry of Massachusetts, Ellsworth of Connecticut, Yates of New York, Paterson of New Jersey, Franklin of Pennsylvania, Bedford of Delaware, Martin of Maryland, Mason of Virginia, Davie of North Carolina, Rutledge of South Carolina, Baldwin of Georgia — a total of eleven, one delegate from each state present at the convention. The New Hampshire delegates still had not reached Philadelphia.

GUNNING BEDFORD

One-State, One-Vote Crusader

Gunning Bedford was the champion of the small states at the Constitutional Convention. He was Delaware's delegate and he followed to the letter Delaware's instructions to insist upon one vote for each state in the national legislature. The compromise which gave all states an equal vote in the Senate was due in part to Bedford.

Bedford was less successful in other campaigns during the convention. He wanted the state legislatures to have power to remove the President. And he wanted the President to serve a term of three years and then be ineligible for re-election for nine years. But when the Constitution was completed, Bedford signed it and supported it in Delaware — helping make Delaware the first state to ratify it.

Born in Philadelphia in 1747, Bedford was graduated from the College of New Jersey (now Princeton) in the same class with James Madison. He moved to Delaware and settled on a farm on the Brandywine River.

During the 1780's Bedford served in his state legislature, in the Continental Congress, and at the Annapolis Convention as well as at the Constitutional Convention.

In 1789 President Washington appointed him a judge for the Delaware district. He served until his death in 1812.

The eleven-member committee was to meet the next day. Meanwhile the convention adjourned for a few days, giving the committee a chance to deliberate and the other delegates a chance to relax over the July 4 holiday.

All over the country people celebrated Independence Day with an already traditional thirteen toasts to the thirteen states. On this eleventh anniversary celebration, many also toasted the still secret convention in Philadelphia. Because of the rule of secrecy, the people knew nothing of the struggle going on there. But many hoped and expected that a constitution would emerge by the time the meeting ended.

The Committee's Compromise

The committee met July 3 with Elbridge Gerry of Massachusetts acting as chairman. Each committee member carried the convictions of his state with him into the meeting. Most members of the committee, like most states, wanted representation in both houses to be based on population. The remainder of the committee, those from small states, wanted an equal number of representatives from each state in both houses. The debate was heated and the vote close, but the committee forged a compromise.

In the first branch each state was to have one representative for every 40,000 people in the state (counting three fifths of the Negro slaves). A state with fewer than 40,000 people would have one representative.

In the Senate each state was to have an equal vote.

Bills for raising money or appropriating it, as well as paying salaries to federal officials, were to originate in the first branch. The Senate could not amend or alter a money bill.

The compromise gave the small states equal representation in the Senate and the big states proportional repre-

ELBRIDGE GERRY
Pro-Federation, Anti-Constitution

To "gerrymander" means to redraw voting district lines in such a way that most opposition voters are in one or two districts, and supporters of the party in power predominate in the other districts. This practice got its name in 1812 when Governor Elbridge Gerry of Massachusetts signed a reapportionment bill creating a voting district of grotesque proportion. The painter, Gilbert Stuart, saw a map of this district, added head, wings, and claws, and remarked, "That will do for a salamander." "Better say Gerrymander," said someone else, and the word was created.

Gerry was born in Marblehead, Massachusetts, in 1744. His father was a prosperous merchant, and young Elbridge followed in his steps. During the Revolution Gerry helped keep the army supplied with munitions and equipment. But people laughed when they heard he fled from a British search party dressed only in his nightshirt.

Although Gerry had urged a strong federal government, he thought the convention had gone too far and he refused to sign the constitution.

Gerry was elected to the U.S. House of Representatives in 1789, to the Governorship of Massachusetts in 1810, and to the Vice-Presidency of the U.S. in 1812. He died in Washington in 1814.

sentation in the first branch where money matters would be handled.

When the convention reopened for business on Thursday, July 5, Gerry presented the committee's compromise. Almost immediately the delegates plunged into bitter debate.

The committee had asked the convention to vote on all provisions of the compromise at once. As a unit, it contained something for all factions. But the delegates insisted upon debating the clauses one by one. They proceeded to take the compromise apart.

Madison Objects

Madison rose to object to equal representation in the Senate. His language was courtly, but his meaning was plain. The compromise was a surrender to the minority, he said. He did not believe Delaware would "brave the consequences of seeking her fortunes apart from the other states" or "pursue the rash policy of courting foreign support."

"Harmony in the convention was no doubt much to be desired," he continued, and satisfying all the states was important. But if the "principal states comprehending a majority of the people" were satisfied with a plan, then the smaller states would "by degrees accede to it."

Gouverneur Morris of Pennsylvania agreed with Madison. He did not think the small states would walk out of the Union. "This country must be united," he declared dramatically. "If persuasion does not unite it, the sword will."

Despite these strong statements the convention voted to let the Senate clause of the compromise stand — for the time being.

On the clause providing that money bills originate in the first branch there was also a heated debate. Wilson of

Pennsylvania thought that the clause was meaningless since the Senate would have to approve money bills before they became law. Gouverneur Morris thought that the Senate would be the superior body and that its abilities ought to be used in devising money bills. Franklin finally took the floor. "The people should know who had disposed of their money and how it had been disposed of," he said. "This end would be best attained if money affairs were to be confined to the immediate representatives of the people." When this clause of the compromise came to a preliminary vote, it too passed.

People or Property

One clause in the compromise remained to be debated — that each state be allowed one member in the first branch for every 40,000 people in the state including three fifths of the Negro slaves. This clause was to provide the most heated debate of all — and a debate with a difference. For the division was not between the big states and the small ones as it had been in most debates so far. The small states had what they wanted in the proposed compromise: equal representation in the Senate. They would accept the rest of the compromise if necessary. Now the split was between states that favored proportional representation based on population alone and states that wanted property included as well.

Gouverneur Morris of Pennsylvania began the debate by calling for proportional representation based on property. Life and liberty might be the first wants of savages, said Morris, but in a civilized society "property was the main object."

Morris, Rutledge of South Carolina, and others who supported property over population as the basis of proportional representation, were speaking for the landowners of the North and the slave owners of the South who would be paying the most in taxes. They were also concerned about new states to be formed out of the western territories. Because many settlers were moving west, the new states would have large populations and might soon be able to outvote eastern states in the legislature if representation were based on population.

When the seriousness of this new rift became clear, the convention turned the question of representation in the first branch over to a small committee. The committee soon came back with a vague solution. It allotted specific numbers of seats to each state ranging from one (for Delaware) to nine (for Virginia). Then it said that in the future the national legislature should have the power to determine the number of representatives any new state should have "upon the principles of their wealth and number of inhabitants."

This compromise on a compromise settled nothing. An-

Rapid growth of settlements west of the Appalachians in the late 1700's promised an influx of new states into the Union.

other committee was appointed, and another allotment drawn up with the same discouraging result.

How to Count Slaves

Both the northern states and the southern states thought they were being discriminated against. The North pointed out that the four New England states had a larger white population than the southern states, but they would have fewer representatives than the South because southern states would be allowed to count their slaves. If property (slaves) was to be counted at all, northerners thought, then they should be allowed to count their ships and shops. The southern states disagreed on whether slaves should be considered as people or wealth for purposes of representation, but they all insisted that they be counted one way or another. They needed the additional representatives in the first branch to stave off any attempt to outlaw slavery.

For days the delegates wrangled. Finally Wilson of Pennsylvania pointed out that the most populous states were also the wealthiest. It would not matter whether people or people and wealth were used as a basis for representation because the result would be about the same. And it would be easier to count people. "Numbers were surely the natural and precise measure of representation. And with respect to property, they could not vary much from the precise measure."

Western Representation

Wilson also pointed out to the delegates that if the western states were large in population, then they deserved a large contingent of representatives in the first branch. "The majority of the people wherever found ought in all questions to govern the minority."

But the southern states were still not willing to give in

unless some slaves were counted. And the northerners knew they would have to give a little in order to keep southerners at the convention.

Three-Fifths Compromise

In the end the delegates settled on the old three-fifths compromise they were all so familiar with. In an almost unanimous vote, they voted to delete wealth (except three fifths of the slaves) as a basis for computing representation in the first branch. They decided to retain the allotments worked out by the last committee because of a lack of information on exact populations. But in the future, they decided, representation and taxation would be based on population including three fifths of the slaves. Population would be determined by a census to be taken every ten years.

The Crucial Vote

By now the convention had gone over all the clauses of the compromise. The delegates had made a few changes, but generally it stood about as it had in the beginning. The whole compromise was now put to the crucial vote.

Five states, Connecticut, New Jersey, Delaware, Maryland, and North Carolina, voted for the compromise. Four, Pennsylvania, Virginia, South Carolina, and Georgia, voted against it. Massachusetts split. The ayes had it, but barely. And the nays were unwilling to accept their defeat. The convention was now hopelessly deadlocked.

Small state delegates began talking about going home. All the delegates knew that if they adjourned, they would never convene again. Yet they despaired of ever finding a way out of the impasse. Perhaps it just was not possible to write a constitution acceptable to all the states and the people. Maybe the Union would just have to fall apart. The mood was one of gloom and despair.

The Federal Compromise

Then, in a quiet, informal, early morning meeting, the corner was turned. Madison describes it briefly in his notes. A group of delegates from the larger states and a few others gathered "before the hour of the convention" in the chamber where they had been meeting. They agreed that there was no chance of budging the small states on equal representation in the Senate. If the convention was to go on and the constitution written, the big states would have to accept the compromise.

That was all there was to the meeting. There was no written agreement, no proposal, no formal record. But from then on the deadlock was broken. The small states, assured that the question of the Senate was settled, talked no more of leaving. There were more debates to come, but no more impasses. From that moment on, all cooperated to work out the details.

This compromise between the nationalists and the confederationists is known as the Great Compromise, or the Federal Compromise. The small states had given up equal representation in the first branch but gained it in the Senate. The big states had gained proportional representation in the first branch and lost it in the Senate. The compromise meant that the U.S. government would be based partly on states and partly on people.

It was the middle of July. The convention had been at work for about seven weeks — hot, hard weeks of argument and hostility, of bitter words and harsh threats. Slowly, however, almost all the delegates had come to realize that the states could not survive independently, that there must be union, and that the only basis for union was the compromise they had just worked out.

The foundation had been laid. From now on it was to be a daily grind of details. Bit by bit, the constitution of the United States was now to be constructed.

Chapter

7

Settling Details

With the make-up of the two legislative houses settled, the convention turned to legislative powers — a far less explosive issue. Bedford of Delaware proposed that the legislature have the power "to legislate in all cases for the general interests of the union, and also in those to which the states are separately incompetent, or in which the harmony of the United States may be interrupted by the exercise of individual legislation." The motion carried.

Next the delegates reversed an earlier decision to let the national legislature veto state laws. Instead they passed a resolution making treaties and laws passed by the U.S. legislature the supreme law of the land. State courts were to be "bound thereby in their decisions," regardless of state law.

This provision was later rewritten to make the Constitution the supreme law of the land. Together with the Judiciary Act of 1789, which provided for appeals from state to federal courts, it formed the barrier that would keep the states from usurping the power of the national government.

With optimism in the air, the convention turned now

to the executive branch. The delegates decided with dispatch that the executive should be "a single person" and that his job should be to execute the national laws. But how was he to be chosen?

Choosing the President

The revised Virginia Plan called for the national legislature to choose the executive, but several delegates objected. Gouverneur Morris of Pennsylvania thought the people should elect the executive. Martin of Maryland suggested that the state legislatures choose electors to do so instead.

The convention was gradually working towards a decision that would let electors, chosen for that purpose, name the executive. But at this point the delegates were not ready to decide how the electors themselves were to be chosen. They returned to the Virginia Plan, which proposed that the national legislature be given the power to name the executive.

Length of term and eligibility for a second term also received lengthy discussion. On length of term, opinions ranged from six years to "during good behavior." The compromise was seven years (it was later changed). Eligibility for a second term turned out to be a knottier problem. If the executive were eligible for a second term, he might spend his first term courting the legislature to ensure re-election. If he was not eligible for a second term, there would be less incentive to do a good job. After wrestling with this problem for some time, the delegates put off a final decision and went on to the judiciary.

The Supreme Court

The committee of the whole had proposed that there be "one supreme tribunal," and the convention now unanimously agreed to the proposal. But how was this

U.S. supreme court to be chosen, and what would its jurisdiction be? Should there be inferior U.S. courts within the states? These were the questions the delegates were to grapple with next.

On the question of appointment, some delegates thought the executive should nominate judges and the Senate approve them (the system finally adopted). But others insisted that the executive alone should have the power. The revised Virginia Plan had proposed that the Senate name judges, and the convention finally voted to follow this suggestion — only to change its mind later. The problem of inferior courts was resolved by a decision to give the legislature authority, but not a mandate, to establish lower courts.

The jurisdiction of the U.S. supreme court and inferior courts would extend to "cases arising under laws passed by the general legislature and to such others as involved the national peace and harmony," the convention decided. The court was therefore to be a working partner with the national legislature and the national executive, a member of a trio, each member of which would effectively check and balance the others.

Judicial Review

In all this discussion of the supreme court, nothing was said about granting the court the power to decide whether an act of Congress was in accord with the Constitution. This power of judicial review was an implied power. It came into being later when the powers of Congress itself were spelled out. When Congressional powers were defined and limited, a necessary implication grew up that some other body — the U.S. Supreme Court — had to enforce the limitations.

On July 23 the two delegates from New Hampshire finally arrived. John Langdon and Nicholas Gilman had not come until now because their state could find no money to pay their way. Langdon, a wealthy and public-spirited businessman, finally furnished the funds for Gilman and himself.

Who Should Ratify the Constitution?

On July 23 the convention also debated the question of who was to ratify (approve) the constitution when it was completed. Some delegates argued that the state legislatures should ratify it. Others said that the people themselves, in conventions called just for that purpose, should do the job. The latter group won the debate.

It was an important victory. For one thing, it improved the chances that the new constitution would be ratified. The state legislatures — whose powers would be cut considerably by the national charter — were bound to oppose it. For another, having the people ratify the constitution underscored an important point — the constitution did not propose a league of states, as the Articles of Confederation did, but a union of the people themselves.

Ten-Day Break

It was now July 26, and the convention had discussed, debated, and in most cases voted on all the resolutions of the Virginia Plan as reported to it by the committee of the whole. It was decided to adjourn the meeting for ten days. The reason, the newspapers were told, was "to give a committee, appointed for the purpose, time to arrange and systematize the materials. . . ."

The committee was made up of Rutledge of South Carolina, Randolph of Virginia, Gorham of Massachusetts, Ellsworth of Connecticut, and Wilson of Pennsylvania. They were to construct a constitution out of all the motions and resolutions that had been accepted by the convention since May 25.

JAMES WILSON
Expert
Constitutionalist

A lawyer by profession, James Wilson was second only to Madison as a constitutional expert. He was one of the few delegates who fully realized that loyalty to nation must come first, but that loyalty to state must not be forgotten. He knew how the Constitution would affect American industry and trade. And he sensed that the United States, governed under the Constitution, could have a magnificent future.

Wilson was born in 1742 in Scotland. He was educated in Scottish schools and came to America when he was twenty-three. After studying law, he set up practice at Carlisle, Pennsylvania.

Elected to the First Continental Congress, Wilson wrote and distributed a pamphlet in which he contended that the British Parliament had no authority over the American colonies. Wilson's resentment of Parliament's domination cooled, but in 1776 he voted for independence. Afterwards, he worked in Congress to strengthen the national government. He was re-elected to Congress several times in the 1780's.

Wilson's eloquence and logic during the Constitutional Convention are described in the text. In 1789 he became an Associate Justice of the U.S. Supreme Court. But his land speculations caught up with him; there was public discredit and talk of impeachment. He died in 1798.

During the ten-day break Washington went fishing at Valley Forge and Trenton, amid scenes that recalled memorable days of the Revolution. Several delegates went home. Others stayed in Philadelphia. Some spent the time reading books lent to the convention by the Library Company, which Franklin had helped found more than fifty years before. They might also have attended the so-called opera house, seeing plays put on by a company of actors from New York.

General Washington spent the bitter winter of 1777-78 with his Revolutionary War soldiers at Valley Forge, Pennsylvania. Here he is shown with his wife on Christmas Day.

Filling in the Details

Meanwhile, the committee — called the Committee of Detail — forged ahead with the task of turning a loose bundle of proceedings into a tightly woven constitution.

Although committee members had been charged with responsibility for arranging and systematizing the materials the convention had collected, they did a great deal more. Where the convention had left gaps, the committee filled them in; where the convention had stated intent, the committee spelled out rules and procedures.

It was the Committee of Detail that worked out many of the requirements for office, for example. It established official names — "Congress," the "House of Representatives," the "Supreme Court," and the "President of the United States of America." It even listed the specific areas in which Congress would have power to legislate.

As a general guide, the committee used the resolutions of the Virginia Plan as amended and passed by the convention. It also drew on the New Jersey Plan and several state constitutions. And some of the ideas were the committee's own.

On August 6 the Committee of Detail presented to the convention a draft containing twenty-three articles, of which seven were further divided into forty-one sections.

The transformation from vaguely worded resolutions into a precisely worded constitution startled many of the delegates. After the draft had been read, the convention adjourned for the rest of the day to give everyone a chance to study it. By the next morning the delegates were ready to begin the painstaking job of going through the document clause by clause.

The first big debate came over the question of who was to be allowed to vote for members of the House of Representatives. The draft stated that those who could vote for members of the most numerous branch of the state legislature could also vote for members of the House of Representatives. Gouverneur Morris and others argued that only landowners should have the vote. Franklin and his supporters pleaded that every man should be able to cast his ballot.

Franklin drove his point home by telling how American

sailors captured by the British during the Revolution chose prison rather than serving on British ships against fellow Americans. British sailors, on the other hand, usually agreed to serve on U.S. ships rather than go to prison, even though these ships were attacking the British. Franklin's point was that men were more likely to be patriotic in a country without class lines or special privilege based on property. The way to insure patriotism, Franklin was saying, was to let all men vote.

Heeding Franklin, the convention refused to make ownership of property a requirement for voting. It even went a step further and refused to say that men must own property before they could run for Congress. It then passed the clause in the proposed constitution as it stood.

Money Bills

Should the House of Representatives have the power to originate money bills? In the Great Compromise, which had been worked out the month before (see p. 95), the small states had won equal representation in the Senate — partly by giving in to the larger states on this matter. The compromise had been written into the proposed constitution.

But now the smaller states were balking. They wanted the Senate (where small states had the same vote as the large ones) to have a hand in raising money. The discussion dragged on until September 8. Finally it was decided that money bills would start in the House, but the Senate could add amendments to the bills — just as it could amend any other bill originating in the House.

The Presidency

The President's powers and duties were debated on and off all through the rest of the convention. The Committee of Detail had followed the convention decisions closely:

the executive was to be chosen by the legislature for a seven-year term, with no re-election. Upon reconsidering, the convention changed its mind. Gradually the delegates decided that the President should be elected, not by Congress as earlier planned, but by electors chosen for that purpose within the states; that his term should be four years; and that he should be eligible for re-election for a second term. He was to be at least thirty-five years old and a "natural born citizen, or a citizen of the United States at the time of the adoption of this Constitution." He was to be commander in chief of the armed forces. He was to have power to make treaties and to appoint diplomats, other U.S. officials, and Supreme Court justices — all with the "advice and consent" of the Senate.

The Presidency, as finally outlined by the convention, was something new in the U.S. government. Under the Articles of Confederation there had been a presiding officer in Congress, but he had no real power. Now the President would have power to veto an act of Congress. The veto would hold unless the act was repassed, this time by a vote of two thirds of the members of each house of Congress. Thus the President would not be elected simply to carry out the laws passed by Congress. With the veto power, he had a strong influence on the making of the laws as well.

Powers of Congress

Under the proposed new constitution, Congress too would be made more powerful, especially in raising money. Under the Articles of Confederation, for example, Congress could only set a tax quota for each state — then hope that the states would tax their people and turn over the tax money to the national treasury. Now Congress had the power to impose taxes directly on the people and to collect from them.

Congress also gained the power to coin money, a power which the states had been exercising and which was now specifically prohibited to them.

The proposed constitution also gave Congress the power to issue paper currency. But the convention rejected this clause. During the Revolutionary War, the Continental Congress had printed paper money with no gold or silver backing in the treasury. The money soon lost all its value, giving rise to the phrase "not worth a continental." After the war several of the states had followed suit and issued their own equally worthless paper money. The delegates feared that the new Congress might be tempted to issue worthless money too. They knew that the task of restoring value to money was long overdue.

Export Duties

The new constitution would also remove from the states and give to Congress the power to tax imports. But it specifically forbade Congress to levy export duties.

The ban on export duties was a concession to the South which depended heavily on exports of farm products for its cash income. An export duty, the South had said, would raise prices and discourage foreign countries from buying. But Congress, controlled in part by northern manufacturing states, might be tempted to tax southern exports for the revenue such a tax would bring in.

Two other concessions to the South were also included. One clause stated that "importation of such persons as the several states shall think proper to admit" shall not be prohibited nor should importations of such persons be taxed. The "persons" were slaves. The other required a two-thirds vote in Congress, rather than a simple majority, to pass navigation acts. The South feared that northern shipowners would press for a law requiring U.S. goods

JOHN RUTLEDGE
He Defended Slavery

At eighteen John Rutledge was sent to London to study. There he developed a love for law and a dislike for British policy. He returned to South Carolina and soon was a prosperous lawyer and Attorney General of the province.

Rutledge was a member of the Stamp Act Congress in 1765. Nine years later he was a member of the Continental Congress. He helped draft the state's first constitution and served in the Provincial Congress which adopted it.

Rutledge was Governor of South Carolina when British forces took possession of the state in 1779. He escaped and helped organize an army to drive the British out. He also restored civil government to South Carolina.

As one of South Carolina's delegates to the Constitutional Convention, Rutledge protested vigorously against the antislavery moves made by delegates from northern states. He saw no wrong in slavery. In the end, however, he signed the Constitution and worked for its ratification.

Rutledge served as South Carolina's Chief Justice until President Washington chose him to succeed John Jay as U.S. Chief Justice. But the U.S. Senate refused to consent to his appointment primarily because of his attacks upon Jay's treaty settling grievances against Britain. He died in 1800 at the age of sixty.

to be transported on U.S. ships with rates higher than those charged by foreign carriers.

Northern delegates opposed all three of these provisions and argued against them. Madison insisted that the national government should have the export taxing privilege. The convention, he said, ought to be "governed by national and permanent views" and not by what a few states wanted. Wilson backed Madison. He said that if Congress could tax imports but not exports, it was taking away from the "common government half the regulation of trade."

Importing Slaves

On the slave trade, the debate was more heated. Martin of Maryland — his state, though southern, had already banned importation of slaves — wanted the importation of slaves to be taxed. Three fifths of the slaves, he noted, were to be counted as people for the purpose of allotting seats in the House of Representatives to the states. If the southern states could import slaves duty free they might build up their slave populations in order to win addi-

BETTMANN ARCHIVE

Importing of slaves from Africa to the United States was legal until Congress banned the practice in 1808 (see p. 151).

tional seats. Furthermore, slavery was wrong from a religious and humanitarian point of view, and it was also dangerous, because the slaves might some day revolt. An import tax on slaves would tend to hold down the number of new slaves brought into the country.

Speaking slowly and precisely (contrary to his usual rapid-fire delivery), Rutledge of South Carolina rose to answer Martin. There was no danger of a revolt, he insisted. Nor did religion or humanity have anything to do with the question. The only thing that mattered, he said, was "interest." "If the northern states consult their interest, they will not oppose the increase of slaves which will increase the commodities of which they will become the carriers." In other words, more slaves would mean

Agriculture was the mainstay of the South's economy, and farmers were becoming more and more dependent on slave labor.

more southern farm products for northern ships to transport. Southern plantation owners and northern shipowners would have more profits.

Ellsworth of Connecticut, a northern state, agreed with Rutledge. "Let every state import what it pleases," he said. "The morality or wisdom of slavery are considerations belonging to the states themselves." Charles Pinckney of South Carolina declared that his state could never accept the constitution if it banned the slave trade.

Like Maryland, Virginia had a law prohibiting slave imports. Mason rose to protest importation of more slaves. "Slavery discourages arts and manufactures," he protested. "The poor despise labor when performed by slaves." Slavery produces "the most pernicious effect on manners. Every master of slaves is born a petty tyrant." Mason demanded that the federal government be granted power to prevent the spread of slavery.

Ellsworth of Connecticut and the two Pinckneys of South Carolina replied. The debate went on and on, and for a while the convention seemed on the verge of deadlock again. The solution — one that had proved effective before — was to turn the problem over to a committee.

On August 24 the committee returned with a compromise the convention found acceptable. It provided that Congress could not prohibit the migration or importation of slaves for twenty years, but a duty like that charged on other imports would have to be paid on imported slaves. A simple majority in Congress could pass navigation acts. And export duties were banned. To this day the United States does not impose any duty on exports.

Decisions

As August drew to a close the convention ticked off article after article of the constitutional draft. Included were articles which:

GOUVERNEUR MORRIS
Constitution Writer

One-legged Gouverneur Morris — he'd lost the other in an accident and stumped around on a peg leg — was a talker. And a fine mind was behind his skill with words. So impressed were the convention delegates that they chose him to put their ideas for a constitution into words.

Morris was born at the family's New York estate in 1752. He was graduated from King's College (now Columbia University) and established a law practice. Something of a loyalist at first, he became a nationalist firebrand.

In 1776 Morris helped draft New York's constitution. In 1778 he was in the Continental Congress in Philadelphia and active on many committees. Defeated for reelection to Congress in 1779, Morris decided to move to Philadelphia. Before long, Robert Morris, then Superintendent of Finance for Congress, chose Gouverneur Morris as his second-in-command (the two were not related). Gouverneur Morris helped plan the decimal coinage system.

In Europe as Robert Morris's business agent in 1789, Morris saw the French Revolution begin. After Jefferson left Paris, he was the most important American in France.

Last of Morris's public offices was that of U.S. Senator from New York, 1800-1803. He died in 1816.

1. Provided for admission by Congress of new states into the Union.

2. Gave the U.S. government power to guarantee a republican form of government to each state and protect it from invasion; and provided that federal forces could be sent into a state if there was serious "domestic violence" and the state asked for help.

3. Provided that ratification of the constitution by nine of the thirteen states would be enough to make the constitution the law of the land.

4. Authorized Congress to establish a federal district to become the seat of the U.S. government.

Committee of Style

With the job of constructing a constitution almost done, the convention appointed a Committee of Style to put the document into final shape. Johnson of Connecticut was chairman. Other committee members were Hamilton of New York, Gouverneur Morris of Pennsylvania, Madison of Virginia, and King of Massachusetts.

Gouverneur Morris did the actual writing of the U.S. Constitution. The other committee members went over it point by point, however, and did not accept Morris' draft until they were completely satisfied with it.

One phrase the committee reworked was the opening statement of the preamble. As written by the Committee of Detail the preamble began: "We, the people of the states of . . ." (naming all the states). The Committee of Style rewrote the preamble to read: "We, the People of the United States, in order to form a more perfect union, establish justice, insure domestic tranquility, provide for the common defence, promote the general welfare, and secure the blessings of liberty to ourselves and our posterity, do ordain and establish this Constitution for the United States of America."

The committee had a practical reason for changing the opening phrase. When the draft of August 6 was submitted, the committee had thought that all the states would have to ratify the constitution before it could be accepted. Hence all the states were named. The final draft specified that ratification by only nine states was necessary. Nobody knew which states would make up the first nine to ratify. The committee therefore sidestepped the question by lumping them all together.

Yet the changed wording has also served another purpose. For the opening phrase has come to mean that the Constitution is by and for the people of a truly united United States, rather than by and for a people who are loyal first to the individual states and second to the United States.

On September 12 Committee Chairman Johnson presented the draft to the convention, and over the next few days the delegates went through it together. But by now they were too impatient to quibble over wording. This draft was to be the final one. With a few minor changes it was to become the Constitution of the United States as we know it today.

Bill of Rights

Many people who read about the convention have asked: "Why didn't the convention consider putting a bill of rights directly into the Constitution?" Mason of Virginia did think the document needed such a bill. Gerry of Massachusetts made a motion to add a bill of rights, and Mason seconded it. But the motion was roundly defeated. The delegates were sure that the bills of rights in the state constitutions were guarantee enough. They did not foresee that lack of such a bill in the U.S. Constitution would work against it during the debates over ratification.

Chapter

8

The Delegates Sign,
the States Ratify

It was the afternoon of Saturday, September 15. The sultry midsummer days were over, and the first fine hints of golden autumn were in the air. The constitutional convention had been hard at work for nearly four months, and its task was almost completed. The delegates would soon return to their home states with a constitution to be debated and finally ratified.

Last Dissension

Most of the delegates at the convention were satisfied that the constitution they had written was the best one they could draw up. It was full of compromises, and probably no one was completely satisfied. But most were now willing to accept it and support it, although even in these closing hours there were still a few dissenting voices.

Randolph of Virginia — the man who had first presented the Virginia Plan — was one of the dissenters. Slowly Randolph had come to doubt the wisdom of the constitution, and he would not sign the document as it stood. He proposed that state conventions discuss the document and offer amendments. Then a second constitutional convention would meet to "reject or incorporate" these amendments.

Mason of Virginia seconded Randolph's proposal. Mason had been angered by what he later described as the "precipitate and intemperate, not to say indecent" rush of the past week to get the job done. Mason was also aroused because the constitution "had been formed without the knowledge or idea of the people. . . . It is improper to say to the people, take this or nothing." And he was known to believe that the constitution should include a bill of rights and that it should not permit more slaves to be imported.

Elbridge Gerry of Massachusetts had his own set of objections. There were some articles of the constitution he did not like but would accept. There were others that he could not accept under any circumstances. He could not, for example, approve of Congress having power to make any law "they may please to call necessary and proper," and to raise money or armed forces "without limit." Nor could he grant the Supreme Court the power to hold a trial without a jury of citizens.

But these dissenters were alone. Their objections were quickly voted down. When the whole constitution was put to a final vote, all states present voted "aye." Madison's record notes: "The Constitution was then ordered to be engrossed, and the House adjourned."

On Monday, September 17, the convention met for the last time. The meeting opened with a reading of the engrossed (neatly copied) constitution. Then Franklin came forward with a message that Wilson read to the delegates. The speech was typical of Franklin — gentle, witty, humane, its points crystal clear.

"Mr. President," Franklin wrote, "I confess that there are several parts of this Constitution which I do not at

GEORGE MASON
Loyal Dissenter

Through most of the Constitutional Convention, George Mason was an active and ardent constitution builder. Yet at the close of the convention he refused to sign the constitution and opposed ratification in Virginia.

Mason's opposition was aroused partly by the absence of a bill of rights. Mason had helped frame Virginia's Declaration of Rights in 1776 and he considered such guarantees vital in the U.S. Constitution as well.

Mason's other objection was to a deal he suspected had been made. In a compromise between North and South the South won a ban on export duties and the North won a limit on the number of years slaves could be imported. Mason was vehemently against slavery. He termed the slave trade "diabolical" and bitterly opposed any compromise extending its life.

Mason was born in 1725 in Fairfax County, Virginia. Privately tutored, he also taught himself by reading in his uncle's library. During the 1750's and 1760's he managed his plantation and served in local government. He was treasurer of the Ohio Company and one of those who authorized George Rogers Clark to conquer the Northwest Territory.

Mason lived to see the Bill of Rights added to the U.S. Constitution. He died shortly afterwards in 1792.

present approve, but I am not sure that I shall never approve them. For, having lived long, I have experienced many instances of being obliged by better information or fuller consideration, to change opinions even on important subjects which I once thought right but found to be otherwise. It is therefore that the older I grow, the more apt I am to doubt my own judgment and to pay more respect to the judgment of others. . . .

"I doubt too whether any other convention we can obtain may be able to make a better Constitution. For when you assemble a number of men to have the advantage of their joint wisdom, you inevitably assemble with those men all their prejudices, their passions, their errors of opinion, their local interests, and their selfish views. From such an assembly can a perfect production be assembled? It therefore astonishes me, sir, to find this system approaching so near to perfection as it does. . . . Thus I consent, sir, to this Constitution because I expect no better, and because I am not sure, that it is not the best. . . .

"On the whole, sir, I cannot help expressing a wish that every member of the convention who may still have objections to it, would with me, on this occasion, doubt a little of his own infallibility — and to make manifest our unanimity, put his name to this instrument."

Other leading delegates, Gouverneur Morris and Hamilton among them, rose to second Franklin's request. Morris said he was ready to sign the constitution "with all its faults."

Delegates Sign

The delegates had finally said their last. Those who were ready to sign came forward. Washington headed the list. The others followed in the order of the states they represented, north to south. Everyone present — except

Thirty-nine delegates, headed by Washington, signed the Constitution. Every state except Rhode Island was represented.

From the original in the Department of State, Washington.

Gerry, Randolph, and Mason — affixed their signatures. There were thirty-nine signers in all and three present who did not sign.

The remaining thirteen of the fifty-five delegates who had originally attended the convention had walked out in protest at various times before the signing ceremony. Now they were at home ready to work against ratification of the constitution. These delegates could spell trouble. But in Independence Hall everything seemed peaceful and optimistic.

A Rising Sun

Madison recorded what Franklin said as the last delegates signed their names: ". . . Franklin looking towards the president's chair, at the back of which a rising sun happened to be painted, observed . . . that painters had found it difficult to distinguish in their art a rising from a setting sun. I have, said he, often and often in the course of the session, and the vicissitudes of my hopes and fears as to its issue, looked at that behind the president without being able to tell whether it was rising or setting. But now at length I have the happiness to know that it is a rising and not a setting sun."

Washington's diary notes the final hours: "The business being thus closed, the members adjourned to the City Tavern, dined together and took a cordial leave of each other; after which I returned to my lodgings . . . and retired to meditate on the momentous work which had been executed, after not less than five, for a large part of the time six, and sometimes seven hours sitting every day, except Sundays and the ten days adjournment to give a committee opportunity and time to arrange the business, for more than four months."

The Constitution had been written, approved, and signed. The work of the Constitutional Convention was over. Now it was time to present it to the people. What would they think of it? More important, would they accept it? Nobody could know the answers.

The Furor Begins

The first step was to submit the proposed Constitution to the old Congress. Along with it went a separate resolution in which the convention recommended that Congress pass the Constitution on to "a convention of delegates, chosen in each state by the peoples thereof . . . for their assent and ratification." It recommended also that as soon as Congress had received notice of ratification from nine states that it should begin proceedings to put the new government into operation.

Congress, meeting in New York City, opened debate on the Constitution on September 26. Active in the discussion were ten convention delegates who were also members of Congress — Langdon and Gilman of New Hampshire, Gorham and King of Massachusetts, Johnson of Connecticut, Madison of Virginia, Blount of North Carolina, Butler of South Carolina, Few and Pierce of Georgia. Together they made up almost one third of the total membership. Enough others rallied to their support to form a majority, and on September 28 Congress agreed to distribute the Constitution to the states without comment.

Copies of the Constitution were also released to the newspapers, and delegates sent it to their friends in foreign countries. Thomas Jefferson, still in Paris, received several copies. Washington, Franklin, Madison, and others each sent him one, eager to know his reaction.

Taking Sides

The people of the various states were not long in lining up either for or against adoption of the Constitution. Supporters were called Federalists, since they stood for a central government sharing power with the states — each type of government to be sovereign in its own sphere. Those opposed soon came to be known as the Anti-Federalists.

The Anti-Federalists were opposed to the Constitution for varying reasons. Some considered the Constitution too weak. Others argued that the United States was already too big to be controlled by a single national government. Many wanted their state governments to retain authority. They were afraid of the taxes and tyrannies a strong central government might impose on them.

The Anti-Federalists, for the most part, wanted the confederation of sovereign states provided for in the Articles of Confederation with, perhaps, the modifications of the New Jersey Plan. As advocates of a decentralized government, they saw dangers in what seemed to them a highly centralized government.

Pennsylvania Debates

Pennsylvania quickly got word that Congress had released the Constitution. On the morning of September 29 the Federalist members of the Pennsylvania Assembly demanded that a date be set for a state convention to meet to ratify the Constitution. The Anti-Federalists wanted more time, and they saw to it that the Assembly was two members shy of a quorum — the minimum number of assemblymen which must be present to take a vote.

The sergeant-at-arms and a clerk went out to round up two more members. They found two Anti-Federalists, but the two refused to come to the chamber. Hearing the refusal, a crowd of Federalists forced the two Anti-Federalists to march to the State House. There the crowd remained until a vote was taken that set the first Tuesday in November as election day for delegates to the state convention.

The Pennsylvania Anti-Federalists were especially loud in their denunciation of the Constitution. They criticized the proposed government as too costly. They said that the U.S. government would side-step the states and rule the people directly and that there was no bill of rights in the Constitution to protect the people. Congress could force the people to pay taxes higher than anyone had ever dreamed of. The President had too much power, and so did the Supreme Court. The House of Representatives had too few members to speak for all the people. The Senate would be made up only of the rich and wellborn. On and on they went.

Wilson Defends the Constitution

James Wilson bore the brunt of the defense. As to the federal government being too powerful, he pointed out that under the Constitution the states would keep for themselves every power not specifically granted to the federal government. Each state had a bill of rights, and a federal bill was not needed. Congress and the President were to be democratically elected. Wilson charged that those who were against the Constitution were mainly state officials who might lose well-paying jobs if the Constitution went into effect.

Wilson carried his fight to the floor of the state convention when it met November 21. "America has it in her power to adopt either of the following modes of government," said Wilson. "She may dissolve the individual sovereignty of the states and become one consolidated empire; she may be divided into thirteen separate, independent, and unconnected commonwealths; she may be erected into two or more confederacies; or lastly, she may become one comprehensive federal republic." This last, Wilson pointed out, was what the Constitutional Convention had chosen as best for the country.

Anti-Federalist Attack

For three weeks a fiery debate continued in the Pennsylvania convention. The Anti-Federalists' attack concentrated on three points:

1. The Constitutional Convention had gone beyond its assignment to revise the Articles of Confederation when it chose to write a new constitution.

2. The new Constitution had no bill of rights.

3. The new Constitution destroyed the sovereignty of the states.

Wilson answered these arguments again and again. The convention *had* gone beyond the strict letter of the assignment, but not beyond what the delegates thought was actually expected of them. No bill of rights was included because each state constitution already had one. The states lost sovereignty only over areas in which the interests of all the people were better served by a federal government.

On December 12 the Pennsylvania state convention finally voted to "assent to and ratify" the Constitution by a vote of 43 to 23. All the Federalists were still for the Constitution; all the Anti-Federalists still against. All the arguments pro and con had swayed neither side.

Delaware First

Despite its head start, Pennsylvania was not the first state to ratify the Constitution. Five days earlier, on December 7, Delaware's convention had unanimously voted to accept the Constitution. Ever since, Delaware has proudly called itself the "First State."

New Jersey and Georgia ratified the Constitution, a few weeks after Pennsylvania had, by unanimous votes. On January 9, 1788, Connecticut voted 128 to 40 for ratification. Massachusetts, spurred by Rufus King, ratified the Constitution on February 6 but by the narrow vote of

RUFUS KING
Stanch Opponent
of Slavery

Like many noted New Yorkers, Rufus King was born elsewhere — in Maine in 1755 when Maine was part of Massachusetts. It was Massachusetts he represented at the Constitutional Convention.

Only thirty-two at the time, King was already a successful attorney and a former member of the Continental Congress. He strongly supported the constitution that emerged, and fought for its ratification in Massachusetts.

King became a New Yorker in 1788, and a year later he was chosen to represent New York in the U.S. Senate. There he was regarded as the ablest Federalist leader of his time. He supported the money policies of Secretary of the Treasury Alexander Hamilton and defended Jay's Treaty with Britain. Possibly as a reward, he was appointed U.S. Minister to Britain and served with distinction for seven years at the Court of St. James's.

King was defeated for the Vice-Presidency in 1804 and 1808, and for the Presidency in 1816. But he was returned to the Senate. In his last years there, King continued the fight against the spread of slavery, a fight that he had begun in the Continental Congress. He had fought against permitting slavery in the Northwest Territory, and later opposed the Missouri Compromise of 1820. He died in 1827.

187 to 168. Maryland (on April 28) and South Carolina (on May 23) also voted "yes." That made eight states — one short of the necessary nine.

New York a Critical State

All eyes turned to New York where opposition was strong and a bitter struggle loomed. It was essential that New York ratify, for without New York the country would be split. Massachusetts, Connecticut, Rhode Island, and New Hampshire on the north would be separated from the rest of the country.

As we have seen, the New York state government was under the control of a political group led by Governor George Clinton. This "Clinton machine" and others vigorously opposed the Constitution because they feared it would reduce the state's independence. Lansing and Yates, two of New York's delegates to the convention, were Clinton men. They had not signed the Constitution and had come home early to fight against its ratification.

Hamilton, New York's third delegate to the Constitutional Convention, was ardently for ratification of the Constitution, and he became the leader of the Federalists in New York. To help win support, Hamilton turned to Madison, who was in New York at the time as a member of Congress, and to John Jay, a New Yorker who had held several high public offices (and was to hold still higher posts).

The Federalist

The weapon these three Federalist leaders chose to use in the struggle was a series of public letters directed to the people of the state of New York. The letters, which came to be known as *The Federalist* papers, explained the proposed Constitution boldly, logically, and truthfully.

Published between the fall of 1787 and the spring of 1788, they appeared two, three, and even four times a week in four different New York City newspapers. All of them were signed "Publius" (a Roman leader who had established a just government), but their readers had a good notion as to the identities of the writers. There were eighty-five letters in all. Hamilton wrote more than half of them, Jay wrote five, and Madison — or Madison and Hamilton together — wrote the rest.

The Federalist papers might have been a series of emotional pleas exhorting readers to back the new Constitution. Instead, they were calm and closely reasoned explanations of the Constitution and the new government it would establish. Their real force lay in their logical presentation, their appeal to practical men. Today, readers marvel at the accuracy with which the papers foretold the way the Constitution would actually work.

When the New York ratifying convention assembled in June 1788, more than two thirds of the delegates were Anti-Federalists. Hamilton insisted that each article of the proposed Constitution be taken up and debated separately. That way he would be able to score points as the debate progressed, and wean support away from the Clinton forces.

New Hampshire

Word arrived that New Hampshire had ratified, bringing the total to nine states. Now New York knew the new government would be formed, whether or not it ratified. Still the debate went on. Finally on July 26 a vote was taken. The result was 30 to 27 in favor of ratification. Hamilton, battling against seemingly overwhelming odds, had won over enough delegates to assure adoption — but by an uncomfortably close margin of three votes.

Virginia Another Critical State

Meanwhile, a bitter struggle was also going on in Virginia, another large and critical state. There the odds were with the Federalists, but the debate was more emotional. Patrick Henry led the Anti-Federalists. Although a stanch patriot during the Revolution, Henry had opposed drafting a new constitution and had refused to serve as a delegate to the Constitutional Convention. Now he thundered for hours on end, day after day against the proposed national charter — principally at its lack of a bill of rights.

"The rights of conscience, trial by jury, liberty of the press, all your communities and franchises, all pretensions to human rights and privileges, are rendered insecure, if not lost, by this change. . . . Is this tame relinquishment of rights worthy of freemen? . . . I would rather infinitely, and I am sure most of this convention are of the same opinion, have a king, lords, and commons, than a government so replete with such insupportable evils," he argued.

George Mason was as outspoken — although not as

Nine states had to ratify the Constitution before it could be put into effect. Soon after this cartoon appeared in a Boston newspaper, New Hampshire, not Virginia, became the ninth.

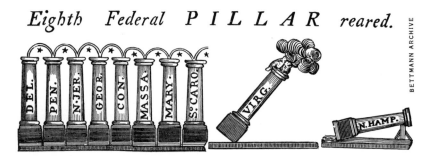

Eighth   Federal   P I L L A R   reared.

BETTMANN ARCHIVE

long-winded. He charged that the federal government was "calculated to annihilate totally the state governments. . . . Is it to be supposed that one national government will suit so extensive a country, embracing so many climates, and containing inhabitants so very different in manners, habits, and customs? Where in history was there any record of so large a country governed without the loss of the people's liberties?"

But Randolph surprised the Virginia convention. He had not signed the Constitution because he wanted it considered by the states, then sent back to a second convention with amendments. But he had come to realize that time was running out. Such a delay would threaten the life of the United States. "I will assent to the lopping of this limb [pointing to his arm]" said he solemnly, "before I assent to the dissolution of the Union."

Madison led the defense. His quiet, reasoned arguments stood in stark contrast to the vivid, impassioned speeches of Patrick Henry. Yet the strongest influence for Virginia's ratification was that of George Washington. His views were known; his prestige was tremendous. A quiet word here and there was enough. When the vote was taken on June 26, the Federalists won. The Constitution was ratified in Virginia 89 to 79.

Last Two to Ratify

North Carolina and Rhode Island were the last to ratify. Both waited until after the new government had been set up. North Carolina had held a convention in July 1788, but it refused to ratify the Constitution. Later, when the new U.S. government began to regard North Carolina as a foreign nation, the state called another convention. Held in November 1789 it accepted the Constitution by a vote of 194 to 77.

Balky Rhode Island — the state which had never sent

delegates to the Constitutional Convention — was the last holdout. Not until May 1790, after the U.S. Senate had passed a bill cutting commercial ties between the United States and Rhode Island, did the state ratify. Even then, ratification squeaked through by a vote of 34 to 32.

Putting the Constitution to Work

On September 13, 1788 — after New Hampshire, Virginia, and New York had voted to ratify the Constitution — Congress set a date in January when the presidential electors were to meet to vote for the President. To nobody's surprise, George Washington was the overwhelming choice for President.

In the meantime the states held elections for members of the House of Representatives, and the state legislatures named their Senators.

Washington Takes Oath

On March 4, 1789, the old Congress declared the new Constitution in effect, thereby putting itself out of business. Not until mid-April, however, were enough newly elected Congressmen assembled in New York to constitute a quorum so the two houses could organize and get down to business. Soon afterwards, on April 30, George Washington was inaugurated as the first President of the United States.

The new Congress, responding to the demand of the state conventions, made it the first order of business to pass ten amendments to the Constitution — the amendments known as the Bill of Rights. The Bill of Rights was ratified by all the states and became part of the Constitution on December 15, 1791.

Many men could take pride in and credit for the giant strides the young United States had taken in the few short years between 1776 when the Declaration of Independence was proclaimed and 1791 when the Bill of Rights was added to the Constitution. In the years ahead many of these same men were to continue to play an invaluable part in shaping the destiny of the United States. They had created a constitution and helped ratify it. Now they were to create a government according to its provisions — to interpret the clauses, to establish procedures, to make it work. The measure of their success may be that the U.S. government still operates on the basis of the Constitution hammered out during the summer of 1787 in Philadelphia. That Constitution is now the oldest written national constitution in the world.

Less than two years after the Convention, Washington was sworn in as the first President under the new Constitution.

Chapter

9

PART II

The Constitution

Then and Now

In the 1780's all of the states of the United States were located largely east of the Appalachians. Most of the area to the west of those mountains was considered wilderness. The fastest means of transportation from one place to another was by horse. Three quarters of the people lived on farms. The largest city, Philadelphia, had a population of about 42,000.

Today, the largest city in the United States, New York, has more than twice the population the entire country had then. The country stretches five thousand miles from New York to Hawaii — a distance covered easily in a few hours by jet. Yet the government of this vast and complex nation draws its authority from words and phrases penned in Philadelphia in the summer of 1787.

How is it possible? Flexibility is the answer. The Constitution has stretched to meet the needs of a growing nation.

The process for amending the Constitution has provided some of the flexibility. But most of the adjustment has come about through a broad interpretation of the original clauses in the Constitution — first by Congress in passing laws, then by the executive branch in administering them, and finally by the Supreme Court in upholding them as being within the meaning and intent of the Constitution.

In the following pages the document itself, in its original form and with the old-fashioned spelling, is set forth.* Sections which have been superseded by amendments are enclosed in brackets. Beneath most of the sections and paragraphs are brief notes giving up-to-date interpretations and some of the laws passed under their authority. Many laws are based on several clauses of the Constitution.

The amendments, starting with the Bill of Rights, are also included. On ratification each has become an integral part of the Constitution. There will be others, just as there will be other and perhaps wider interpretations of the clauses in the body of the Constitution. For this is a living, growing document assuring the rule of law in a vibrant, growing nation.

The text of the United States Constitution follows:

Preamble

We, the People of the United States, in order to form a more perfect union, establish justice, insure domestic tranquility, provide for the common defence, promote the general welfare, and secure the blessings of liberty to ourselves and our posterity, do ordain and establish this Constitution for the United States of America.

The Preamble introduces the Constitution, states its purpose, and names the source of its authority. This last is particularly important, for the Preamble begins "We, the People of the United States," — not "We, the People

*The version of the U.S. Constitution given here is the one reported in House Document No. 189, 88th Congress, 2d Session, 1964.

of the states of . . ." The Constitution derives its authority directly from the people rather than from the states.

Article I

Sect. 1. ALL legislative powers herein granted shall be vested in a Congress of the United States, which shall consist of a Senate and House of Representatives.

Note the words "all" and "herein granted." The first means that Congress, the legislative branch, will make all laws permitted by the Constitution. The administrative and the judicial branches shall make none of them. These latter two branches, however, make rulings and judgments that have the force of law.

The phrase "herein granted" means that Congress may legislate only to carry out those powers granted to it or implied by the Constitution.

Sect. 2. The House of Representatives shall be composed of members chosen every second year by the people of the several states, and the electors in each state shall have the qualifications requisite for electors of the most numerous branch of the state legislature.

The "electors" are the voters. Those who are permitted under state laws to vote for members of the state house of representatives ("the most numerous branch") have the right under the Constitution to vote for members of the U.S. House of Representatives. Thus each state determines qualifications for voting. In setting up qualifications, however, a state may not violate the provisions of Amendment 14 (p. 183), Amendment 15 (p. 186) Amendment 19 (p. 187), and Amendment 24 (p. 192), or the Voting Rights Act of 1965.

No person shall be a representative who shall not have attained to the age of twenty-five years, and been seven years a citizen of the United States, and who shall not, when elected, be an inhabitant of that state in which he shall be chosen.

Sometimes an elected Representative lacks a few weeks of filling the age or length-of-citizenship requirement. He takes the oath of office and is admitted to the House as soon as he does qualify. The Constitution says he must live in the state that chooses him, but not necessarily in the legislative district he represents. In actual practice, it is usually necessary to live in the district to win election.

[Representatives and direct taxes shall be apportioned among the several states which may be included within this Union, according to their respective numbers, which shall be determined by adding to the whole number of free persons, including those bound to service for a term of years, and excluding Indians not taxed, three-fifths of all other persons.] The actual enumeration shall be made within three years after the first meeting of the Congress of the United States, and within every subsequent term of ten years, in such manner as they shall by law direct. The number of representatives shall not exceed one for every thirty thousand, but each state shall have at least one representative; and until such enumeration shall be made, the state of New-Hampshire shall be entitled to chuse three, Massachusetts eight, Rhode-Island and Providence Plantations one, Connecticut five, New-York six, New-Jersey four, Pennsylvania eight, Delaware one, Maryland six, Virginia ten, North-Carolina five, South-Carolina five, and Georgia three.

"Other persons," as we have seen in Part One, meant slaves. Amendments 13 (p. 182) and 14, Section 2 (p. 183) made the sentence enclosed by brackets obsolete.

The "actual enumeration" means the U.S. Census of Population, taken every tenth year. The growth of the U.S. population has made "one Representative for every

30,000" impractical. In recent years Congress has limited the total number of Representatives to 435.

After each census the 435 representatives are reapportioned among the states to reflect population changes. The state legislatures do the actual redrawing of district lines. In the past the party in power in many state legislatures has redrawn district lines in such a way as to preserve its power — with the result that districts within a state have varied widely in population. Since 1964, when the Supreme Court declared this practice unconstitutional, state legislatures have been redistricting to make the districts more equal.

When vacancies happen in the representation from any state, the Executive authority thereof shall issue writs of election to fill such vacancies.

This means that when a Representative dies or resigns in midterm, his state governor must order a special election in his Congressional district to fill his seat. The governor cannot appoint a substitute Representative.

The House of Representatives shall chuse their Speaker and other officers; and shall have the sole power of impeachment.

In actual practice the Speaker of the House is not chosen by the whole House, but by (and from) the members of the majority party in the House. "Power of impeachment" means power to make formal charges against a civilian official of the federal government. The Senate tries impeachments (see p. 139).

Sect. 3. The Senate of the United States shall be composed of two senators from each state, [chosen by the legislature thereof,] for six years; and each senator shall have one vote.

Immediately after they shall be assembled in consequence of the first election, they shall be divided as equally as may be into three classes. The seats of the senators of the first class shall be vacated at the expiration of the second year, of the second class at the expiration of the fourth year, and of the third class at the expiration of the sixth year, so that one-third may be chosen every second year; [and if vacancies happen by resignation, or otherwise, during the recess of the Legislature of any state, the Executive thereof may make temporary appointments until the next meeting of the Legislature, which shall then fill such vacancies.]

No person shall be a senator who shall not have attained to the age of thirty years, and been nine years a citizen of the United States, and who shall not, when elected, be an inhabitant of that state for which he shall be chosen.

The parts enclosed by brackets were changed by Amendment 17 (see p. 186). The division of Senators into three classes works out so that about one third of the Senators are newly elected every two years. One third of the Senators have already served two years of their terms, and one third have served four years.

The Senate, rarely photographed in session, votes its "consent" to President J. F. Kennedy's limited nuclear test ban treaty in 1963.

> The Vice-President of the United States shall be President of the senate, but shall have no vote, unless they be equally divided.

Unlike the Speaker of the House, the President of the Senate (the U.S. Vice-President) has no vote except to break a tie.

> The Senate shall chuse their other officers, and also a President pro tempore, in the absence of the Vice-President, or when he shall exercise the office of President of the United States.

"Pro tempore" is Latin for "for the time being." The President pro tempore presides over the Senate in the absence of the Vice-President. By custom the President pro tempore is the member of the majority party with the greatest number of years of service.

> The Senate shall have the sole power to try all impeachments. When sitting for that purpose, they shall be on oath or affirmation. When the President of the United States is tried, the Chief Justice shall preside: And no person shall be convicted without the concurrence of two-thirds of the members present.
>
> Judgment in cases of impeachment shall not extend further than to removal from office, and disqualification to hold and enjoy any office of honor, trust or profit under the United States; but the party convicted shall nevertheless be liable and subject to indictment, trial, judgment and punishment, according to law.

The House *impeaches* a federal government official; the Senate *tries* him. When the Senate tries a President, the U.S. Chief Justice presides. Only one President, Andrew Johnson, has been impeached. He was tried in 1868 and found not guilty. A federal official convicted under impeachment proceedings may be removed from office and disqualified from holding further office only. But if he has committed a crime, he may also be tried before a regular court of law.

The power to impeach and try federal officials gives the legislature one of its checks on the power of the executive and judicial branches of the government (see p. 155).

Sect. 4. The times, places and manner of holding elections for senators and representatives, shall be prescribed in each state by the legislature thereof; but the Congress may at any time by law make or alter such regulations, except as to the places of chusing Senators.

Under this clause Congress has prescribed that all states hold elections for Senators and Representatives on the first Tuesday after the first Monday in November in even-numbered years. Congress has also limited campaign expenditures. Along with Amendments 14 (p. 183), 15 (p. 186), 17 (p. 186), and 24 (p. 192), and Section 2 of this article, this clause provides the basis for the Civil Rights Act of 1957 and the Voting Rights Act of 1965.

The Congress shall assemble at least once in every year, and such meeting shall [be on the first Monday in December,] unless they shall by law appoint a different day.

The phrase enclosed by the brackets was changed by Amendment 20 (see p. 188).

Sect. 5. Each house shall be the judge of the elections, returns and qualifications of its own members, and a majority of each shall constitute a quorum to do business; but a smaller number may adjourn from day to day, and may be authorized to compel the attendance of absent members, in such manner, and under such penalties as each house may provide.

Each house may determine the rules of its proceedings, punish its members for disorderly behaviour, and, with the concurrence of two-thirds, expel a member.

Congress has interpreted the word "qualifications" to mean moral and political qualifications as well as those qualifications listed in the Constitution. In 1900 the House refused to seat an elected Representative because he was a polygamist (he had several wives) and therefore morally unfit. It refused to seat another Representative because his views were considered "un-American."

A quorum is necessary to take a vote. But a speech or a debate may take place with only a few members (or none other than the speaker) present.

Each house shall keep a journal of its proceedings, and from time to time publish the same, excepting such parts as may in their judgment require secrecy; and the yeas and nays of the members of either house on any question shall, at the desire of one-fifth of those present, be entered on the journal.

Neither house, during the session of Congress, shall, without the consent of the other, adjourn for more than three days, nor to any other place than that in which the two houses shall be sitting.

The *Journal* is the official record of the acts, votes, and resolutions of Congress. The *Congressional Record*, on the other hand, prints what Representatives and Senators say on the floors of their houses. Actually, they can "revise and extend" what they said, so that much of what is in the *Congressional Record* was never heard in Congress.

Sect. 6. The senators and representatives shall receive a compensation for their services, to be ascertained by law, and paid out of the treasury of the United States. They shall in all cases, except treason, felony and breach of the peace, be privileged from arrest during their attendance at the session of their respective houses, and in going to and returning from the same; and for any speech or debate in either house, they shall not be questioned in any other place.

Congressmen are paid $30,000 a year plus various allowances. They cannot be arrested for minor offenses while they are actually carrying out Congressional duties. And they cannot be arrested, tried, or sued at any time for anything they say on the floors of their Houses or in committee meetings. This is a great privilege, which has been used recklessly at times.

No senator or representative shall, during the time for which he was elected, be appointed to any civil office under the authority of the United States, which shall have been created, or the emoluments whereof shall have been encreased during such time; and no person holding any office under the United States, shall be a member of either house during his continuance in office.

Congressmen cannot hold other civil offices in the U.S. government. They can be, and some are, Reserve members of the U.S. armed forces.

Sect. 7. All bills for raising revenue shall originate in the house of representatives; but the senate may propose or concur with amendments as on other bills.

Revenue bills must start in the House. But the Senate, in amending a House revenue bill, can cancel everything except the title and enacting clause, and write its own bill.

Every bill which shall have passed the house of representatives and the senate, shall, before it become a law, be presented to the president of the United States; if he approve he shall sign it, but if not he shall return it, with his objections to that house in which it shall have originated, who shall enter the objections at large on their journal, and proceed to reconsider it. If after such reconsideration two-thirds of that house shall agree to pass the bill, it shall be sent, together with the objections, to the other house, by which it shall likewise be reconsidered, and if approved by two-thirds of that

President Johnson signs the 1965 education bill into law outside his old school in Texas. His first-grade teacher sits beside him.

house, it shall become a law. But in all such cases the votes of both houses shall be determined by yeas and nays, and the names of the persons voting for and against the bill shall be entered on the journal of each house respectively. If any bill shall not be returned by the President within ten days (Sundays excepted) after it shall have been presented to him, the same shall be a law, in like manner as if he had signed it, unless the Congress by their adjournment prevent its return, in which case it shall not be a law.

As part of the checks and balances system, the Constitution gives the President, the chief executive officer, several ways to influence legislation. Through his veto power, for example, he can delay or prevent the passage of a bill. When he disapproves a bill Congress has passed and sent to him, he vetoes it by returning it to Congress unsigned. To overcome the President's veto, both houses must repass the bill by a vote of two thirds of a quorum of members. The President may also register disapproval of a bill through a pocket veto. Instead of returning the bill unsigned, he holds it. If Congress adjourns within ten days, not counting Sundays, the bill does not become law. If Congress does not adjourn, however, the bill automatically becomes law after the ten days are up.

Every order, resolution, or vote to which the concurrence of the Senate and House of Representatives may be necessary (except on a question of adjournment) shall be presented to the President of the United States; and before the same shall take effect, shall be approved by him, or, being disapproved by him, shall be repassed by two-thirds of the Senate and House of Representatives, according to the rules and limitations prescribed in the case of a bill.

This gives the President power to sign or veto other measures that Congress has passed. Certain measures do not require the President's signature. For example, Congress may propose an amendment to the Constitution and submit it to the states for ratification without the President's signature.

Sect. 8. The Congress shall have power

To lay and collect taxes, duties, imposts and excises, to pay the debts and provide for the common defence and general welfare of the United States; but all duties, imposts and excises shall be uniform throughout the United States;

Congress levies indirect taxes in the form of duties, imposts, and excises. Duties and imposts are tariffs on goods shipped to the United States from foreign countries. Excises are taxes on the manufacture or sale of specific items such as liquor and gasoline. The manufacturer or seller pays the tax but he passes the cost along to the buyer.

"Uniform throughout the United States" means that a certain federal tax on an item cannot be charged in one state and a different tax charged on the same item in another state. Direct taxes must be apportioned according to population (see Article I, Section 9, p. 152). The 16th Amendment provides the authority for the income tax (see p. 186).

To borrow money on the credit of the United States;

Congress borrows funds by selling government securities — mainly bonds, treasury certificates, and treasury notes — to banks, other businesses, and individual buyers.

To regulate commerce with foreign nations, and among the several states, and with the Indian tribes;

Regulating commerce with foreign nations gives Congress power to collect tariffs on imports, ban harmful goods, hold goods in the United States that the country needs (especially for defense), and control all types of transportation and communication between the United States and other nations.

Regulating commerce among the states means control of everything that crosses state borders — goods, vehicles, people, communications — and everything within the boundaries of a state that affects interstate commerce.

The commerce clause has been interpreted broadly by the Supreme Court, and Congress has based much legislation on it. Under this clause, for example, Congress has established minimum wage standards to be met in factories producing goods for interstate trade. It has established regulatory agencies such as the Federal Communications Commission which regulates broadcasting, telephone and telegraph operations. And it has passed civil rights legislation banning discrimination in public accommodations. The reasoning behind the public accommodations law: a Negro who is refused a room at a "whites only" hotel may be hampered in his travel from state to state. Travel is considered one form of commerce.

The commerce clause of the U.S. Constitution is the springboard for much federal legislation. It has, for example, enabled Congress to regulate wages and hours in all business enterprises that engage in interstate commerce. Also based on the commerce clause are laws specifying what may or may not be imported into the United States by returning travelers or by foreign trading firms.

To establish an uniform rule of naturalization, and uniform laws on the subject of bankruptcies throughout the United States;

"Naturalization" is the process by which a foreigner becomes a U.S. citizen. "Bankruptcy" is the process by which a man, unable to pay what he owes, gives up his remaining property to his creditors and is freed of obligation to them. Theoretically he is penniless but free of debt and ready to start over.

To coin money, regulate the value thereof, and of foreign coin, and fix the standard of weights and measures;

To provide for the punishment of counterfeiting the securities and current coin of the United States;

Under this clause (and others) Congress not only provides for the minting of metal coins but also charters federal reserve banks which in turn issue paper currency. Congress regulates the value of U.S. currency by deter-

An increasing demand for coins keeps U.S. mints at Denver (above) and Philadelphia busy. The Philadelphia mint was founded in 1792.

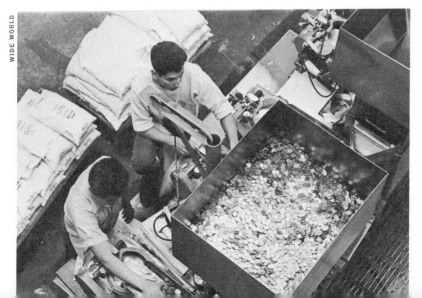

mining how much gold, silver, or U.S. credit backs it. Congress can punish those who make fake U.S. money.

To establish post offices and post roads;

Under this clause, Congress can give money to the states to build and maintain roads. It can also help airlines, railroads, and shipping companies.

To promote the progress of science and useful arts, by securing for limited times to authors and inventors the exclusive right to their respective writings and discoveries;

Writers, composers, and other artists can copyright their works for twenty-eight years and renew the copyright for another twenty-eight years. After that the work is in the "public domain" and may be reproduced by anyone. An inventor can patent his work for a period of seventeen years.

The U.S. postal system with its vast network of offices brings a vital government service into every city and hamlet in the nation.

To constitute tribunals inferior to the supreme court;

The U.S. Supreme Court is established by the Constitution. But Congress establishes all federal courts below the Supreme Court — and has power to abolish them.

To define and punish piracies and felonies committed on the high seas, and offences against the law of nations;

Congress can vote to make an international crime, such as piracy, be considered a national crime as well.

To declare war, grant letters of marque and reprisal, and make rules concerning captures on land and water;

The President can recommend that war be declared — Congress must make the actual declaration. In practice Congress has always acted on the President's recommendation. "Letters of marque and reprisal" were authorizations to private shipowners and their captains to attack ships of enemy nations. The practice has been outlawed by international treaty.

To raise and support armies, but no appropriation of money to that use shall be for a longer term than two years;

To provide and maintain a navy;

To make rules for the government and regulation of the land and naval forces;

To provide for calling forth the militia to execute the laws of the union, suppress insurrections and repel invasions;

To provide for organizing, arming, and disciplining, the militia, and for governing such part of them as may be employed in the service of the United States, reserving to the States respectively, the appointment of the officers, and the authority of training the militia according to the discipline prescribed by Congress;

These clauses give Congress sweeping powers in time of war — including civil war. Under its war power, for example, Congress has established the draft, set price ceil-

After Japan attacked Pearl Harbor in 1941, President Franklin D. Roosevelt went before Congress to ask for a declaration of war.

ings, directed production, rationed consumer goods, and set up the Atomic Energy Commission. The two-year limit on military appropriations is intended to help insure civilian control of the military.

The "militia" is now called the National Guard. In peacetime it operates under the control of the states, with certain directions coming from Congress. A state governor can call out the National Guard in his state in case of trouble. When the federal government calls it out, it becomes part of the U.S. Army.

> To exercise exclusive legislation in all cases whatsoever, over such district (not exceeding ten miles square) as may, by cession of particular States, and the acceptance of Congress, become the seat of the government of the United States, and to exercise like authority over all places purchased by the consent of the legislature of the state in which the same shall be, for the erection of forts, magazines, arsenals, dock-yards, and other needful buildings; — And

Congress acts as city council for the District of Columbia. The President appoints, with Senate approval, three commissioners to administer local laws in the District. "Home rule" for the District is a subject of contention.

> To make all laws which shall be necessary and proper for carrying into execution the foregoing powers, and all other powers vested by this constitution in the government of the United States, or in any department or officer thereof.

"Foregoing powers" and "necessary and proper" are the important phrases here. Congress is not empowered to pass laws for any and all purposes, but only to carry out the "foregoing powers" — those powers specifically delegated to it by the Constitution. The phrase "necessary and proper," however, gives Congress broad scope in exercising these powers. This is the clause which gives Congress *implied powers*. The power to tax and spend for the general welfare, for example, implies the power to spend tax money for highways, school aid, and social security — none of which are mentioned in the Constitution. The Lend-Lease Act of 1941 extending aid to the British Commonwealth was passed under the power of Congress to tax and spend for the national defense. The "necessary and proper" clause has greatly expanded the power of the federal government and has helped keep the Constitution flexible and up-to-date.

> *Sect.* 9. The migration or importation of such persons as any of the states now existing shall think proper to admit, shall not be prohibited by the Congress prior to the year one thousand eight hundred and eight, but a tax or duty may be imposed on such importation, not exceeding ten dollars for each person.

This was the clause that enabled Congress to end the importing of slaves in 1808 (see p. 110).

> The privilege of the writ of habeas corpus shall not be suspended, unless when in cases of rebellion or invasion the public safety may require it.

A writ of habeas corpus (Latin for "you have the body") is a court-issued order requiring an arresting officer to appear before the court and tell why his prisoner is being held. If the officer cannot give a good reason, the judge may order the prisoner to be released. Only in extreme emergencies involving the safety of the general public may the writ be denied. The Constitution does not say *who* has the right to suspend the writ, and the Supreme Court has never decided. Many believe the right belongs to Congress, but President Abraham Lincoln suspended the privilege of the writ during the Civil War.

> No bill of attainder or ex post facto law shall be passed.

A bill of attainder is a law that has the effect of convicting and punishing a person without trial. An ex post facto ("after the fact") law is one making a certain act a crime *after* the act was committed.

> No capitation, or other direct, tax shall be laid, unless in proportion to the census or enumeration herein before directed to be taken.

"Capitation" tax means poll or "head" tax. No such tax may be imposed unless it is apportioned among the states according to population.

The exact meaning of the term "direct tax" has never been defined. For many years Congress relied on indirect taxes such as the excise tax and import duties to provide the bulk of its income. The income tax, first imposed during the Civil War, was at that time considered an indirect tax. Later, the Supreme Court held that the income tax was a direct tax and, therefore, unconstitutional. Finally, Amendment 16 was passed to give Congress the authority to reinstate the income tax without apportioning it among the states according to population (see p. 186).

No tax or duty shall be laid on articles exported from any state. No preference shall be given by any regulation of commerce or revenue to the ports of one state over those of another: nor shall vessels bound to, or from, one state, be obliged to enter, clear, or pay duties in another.

Congress may not levy export tariffs on goods shipped out of the United States. It cannot discriminate against the ports of one state in favor of those of another, and U.S. ships must be allowed to enter all U.S. ports freely.

No money shall be drawn from the treasury, but in consequence of appropriations made by law; and a regular statement and account of the receipts and expenditures of all public money shall be published from time to time.

All parts of the government depend on Congress to appropriate funds for their work. Thus Congress checks and balances the executive and the judiciary branches.

No title of nobility shall be granted by the United States:— And no person holding any office of profit or trust under them, shall, without the consent of the Congress, accept of any present, emolument, office, or title, of any kind whatever, from any king, prince, or foreign state.

Congress cannot grant titles of nobility, nor can any official of the United States accept such an honor from a foreign country without the consent of Congress.

Sect. 10. No state shall enter into any treaty, alliance, or confederation; grant letters of marque and reprisal; coin money; emit bills of credit; make any thing but gold and silver coin a tender in payment of debts; pass any bill of attainder, ex post facto law, or law impairing the obligation of contracts, or grant any title of nobility.

No state shall, without the consent of the Congress, lay any imposts or duties on imports or exports, except what may be absolutely necessary for executing its inspection laws; and the net produce of all duties and imposts, laid by any state on imports or exports, shall be for the use of the Treasury of the United States; and all such laws shall be subject to the revision and controul of the Congress. No state shall, without the consent of Congress, lay any duty of tonnage, keep troops, or ships of war in time of peace, enter into any agreement or compact with another state, or with a foreign power, or engage in war, unless actually invaded, or in such imminent danger as will not admit of delay.

Some of the limitations imposed on the states are also imposed on the federal government. Others, such as the prohibition against making treaties with foreign governments, are intended to keep the states from exercising powers reserved to the federal government.

Interstate compacts are often used as the bases for flood control, conservation, and port development projects. Congress must approve these compacts.

Article II

Sect. 1. The executive power shall be vested in a president of the United States of America. He shall hold his office during the term of four years, and, together with the vice-president, chosen for the same term, be elected as follows.

Article I, Section 1, begins "All legislative powers herein granted shall be vested in a Congress of the United States. . . ." The qualifying phrase "herein granted" is not used in the sentence above describing executive power. This has been taken to mean that the President has general executive power as well as the specific powers granted or implied in the Constitution. He is limited only by the qualifications and exceptions set forth in the Constitution. (See also Amendment 22, p. 191.)

CHECKS AND BALANCES IN THE U.S. GOVERNMENT

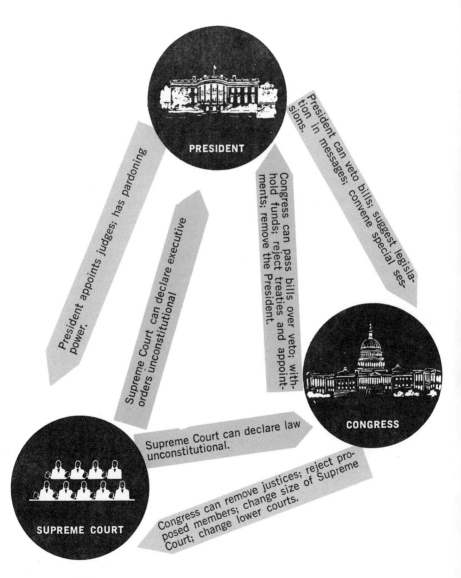

PRESIDENT

President can veto bills; suggest legislation in messages; convene special sessions.

President appoints judges; has pardoning power.

Supreme Court can declare executive orders unconstitutional

Congress can pass bills over veto; withhold funds; reject treaties and appointments; remove the President.

CONGRESS

Supreme Court can declare law unconstitutional.

Congress can remove justices; reject proposed members; change size of Supreme Court; change lower courts.

SUPREME COURT

HOWARD KATZ

Each state shall appoint, in such manner as the legislature thereof may direct, a number of electors, equal to the whole number of senators and representatives to which the state may be entitled in the Congress: but no senator or representative, or person holding an office of trust or profit under the United States, shall be appointed an elector.

When a voter casts his ballot for a Presidential candidate, he is actually voting for a slate of electors pledged to that candidate. Each slate contains the total number of electors to which the state is entitled. The slate with the most votes in each state wins. Thus all the electoral votes in a state go to one candidate (see Amendment 23, p. 191).

[The electors shall meet in their respective states, and vote by ballot for two persons, of whom one at least shall not be an inhabitant of the same state with themselves. And they shall make a list of all the persons voted for, and of the number of votes for each; which list they shall sign and certify, and transmit sealed to the seat of the government of the United States, directed to the president of the senate. The president of the senate shall, in the presence of the senate and house of representatives, open all the certificates, and the votes shall then be counted. The person having the greatest number of votes shall be the president, if such number be a majority of the whole number of electors appointed; and if there be more than one who have such majority, and have an equal number of votes, then the house of representatives shall immediately chuse by ballot one of them for president; and if no person have a majority, then from the five highest on the list the said house shall in like manner chuse the president. But in chusing the president, the votes shall be taken by states, the representation from each state having one vote; a quorum for this purpose shall consist of a member or members from two-thirds of the states, and a majority of all the states shall be necessary to a choice. In every case, after the choice of the president, the person having the greatest number of votes of the electors shall be the vice-president. But if there should remain two or more who have equal votes, the senate shall chuse from them by ballot the vice-president.]

This paragraph has been entirely replaced by Amendment 12 (see p. 179). The change was prompted by the formation of political parties. Under the original system the electors, chosen in the states, were to cast their votes for the two men they thought best suited for the Presidency. The winner was to be President; the runner-up, Vice-President. If a tie occurred, the House of Representatives, voting by states, was to choose. In the election of 1800 the majority of electors chosen were Democratic-Republicans, and in the electoral college each Democratic-Republican elector cast his two votes for the two candidates of his party, Thomas Jefferson and Aaron Burr, thus creating a tie for the Presidency. The House of Representatives had to vote 36 times in order to break the tie. Jefferson became President and Burr Vice-President.

The Congress may determine the time of chusing the electors, and the day on which they shall give their votes; which day shall be the same throughout the United States.

Congress has set the first Tuesday after the first Monday in November in Presidential election years as the day voters choose electors. The electors do not cast their votes, however, until the first Monday after the second Wednesday in December when they assemble, usually in their state capitals. A list of votes is then sent to the President of the Senate (the Vice-President). In January, in front of the whole Congress, he counts the votes. Not until then are the winners formally elected.

No person except a natural born citizen, or a citizen of the United States, at the time of the adoption of this constitution, shall be eligible to the office of president; neither shall any person be eligible to that office who shall not have attained to the age of thirty-five years, and been fourteen years a resident within the United States.

Is a child born abroad of American parents a natural-born citizen? The courts have yet to rule on this question as it affects Presidential eligibility. Franklin D. Roosevelt, Jr., sometimes mentioned for the Presidency, was born at his family's summer home on Campobello, a small Canadian island in the Bay of Fundy. George Romney, Governor of Michigan, and sometimes considered a Presidential possibility, was born in Chihuahua, Mexico.

In case of the removal of the president from office, or of his death, resignation, or inability to discharge the powers and duties of the said office, the same shall devolve on the vice-president, and the Congress may by law provide for the case of removal, death, resignation or inability, both of the president and vice-president, declaring what officer shall then act as president, and such officer shall act accordingly, until the disability be removed, or a president shall be elected.

The proposed 25th Amendment, offered to the states for ratification in 1965, makes specific the somewhat ambiguous language of this paragraph (see p. 192).

The president shall, at stated times, receive for his services, a compensation, which shall neither be encreased nor diminished during the period for which he shall have been elected, and he shall not receive within that period any other emolument from the United States, or any of them.

The President receives a taxable salary of $100,000 a year, a taxable expense allowance of $50,000 a year, and a further nontaxable expense allowance of $40,000 a year. After he leaves office, he gets a lifetime pension of $25,000 a year, free office space and free mailing privileges, and up to $50,000 a year for office assistants. His widow receives a lifetime pension of $10,000 annually.

Before he enter on the execution of his office, he shall take the following oath or affirmation:

"I do solemnly swear (or affirm) that I will faithfully execute the office of president of the United States, and will to the best of my ability, preserve, protect and defend the constitution of the United States."

President Herbert Hoover (1929-1933) was the only President who chose to "affirm" rather than "swear." His Quaker faith did not permit him to "swear." The Chief Justice of the United States usually swears in the President. However, the night President Warren Harding died in 1923, Vice-President Calvin Coolidge was sworn in by his father, a Northampton, Massachusetts, justice of the peace. The swearing-in took place by the light of a kerosene lamp at the family farmhouse.

A federal judge administers the oath of office to Vice-President Johnson after the assassination of President Kennedy in 1963.

President Franklin D. Roosevelt, Commander in Chief of U.S. military forces, inspects troops in North Africa during World War II.

Sect. 2. The president shall be commander in chief of the army and navy of the United States, and of the militia of the several States, when called into the actual service of the United States; he may require the opinion, in writing, of the principal officer in each of the executive departments, upon any subject relating to the duties of their respective offices, and he shall have power to grant reprieves and pardons for offences against the United States, except in cases of impeachment.

As Commander in Chief of all the U.S. armed forces including the Air Force and the National Guard when it is called into federal service, the President shares control over the military with Congress. Congress declares war and appropriates money to fight it, but the President issues orders. Presidents have also assumed broad powers over civilians during wartime under this clause. During World War II President Franklin D. Roosevelt imposed food rationing and travel restrictions on the people.

The clause beginning ". . . he may require the opinion . . ." led to the formation of the President's Cabinet, which now consists of eleven department heads.

He shall have power, by and with the advice and consent of the senate, to make treaties, provided two-thirds of the senators present concur; and he shall nominate, and by and with the advice and consent of the senate, shall appoint ambassadors, other public ministers and consuls, judges of the supreme court, and all other officers of the United States, whose appointments are not herein otherwise provided for, and which shall be established by law. But the Congress may by law vest the appointment of such inferior officers, as they think proper, in the president alone, in the courts of law, or in the heads of departments.

The president shall have power to fill up all vacancies that may happen during the recess of the senate, by granting commissions which shall expire at the end of their next session.

President Johnson consults with "principal officers" of the State and Defense departments and other members of the executive branch.

UPI

The President, through the State Department, ordinarily negotiates treaties with foreign countries. They are then presented to the Senate for approval by a two-thirds majority. Achieving a two-thirds vote in the Senate is sometimes difficult. In such cases, other procedures may be used to make agreements with foreign governments. One is the joint resolution of Congress which requires only a majority vote. The other is the executive agreement made by the President alone. President Franklin D. Roosevelt's 1940 swap of fifty "overage destroyers" with Britain in exchange for leases on military bases was done by executive agreement.

Senators of the same party as the President are granted "Senatorial courtesy" over the President's political appointments in their states. Thus these Senators usually control federal appointments in their own states.

Sect. 3. He shall from time to time give to the Congress information of the state of the union, and recommend to their consideration such measures as he shall judge necessary and expedient; he may, on extraordinary occasions, convene both houses, or either of them, and in case of disagreement between them, with respect to the time of adjournment, he may adjourn them to such time as he shall think proper; he shall receive ambassadors and other public ministers; he shall take care that the laws be faithfully executed, and shall commission all the officers of the United States.

When Congress begins its new session each January, the President delivers his State of the Union address. Soon after, he sends a budget and a general economic message to Congress. As the session progresses, he makes legislative recommendations. A bill must be introduced by a Congressman, but many bills so introduced actually come from the executive branch.

The power to receive ambassadors implies the power

Meeting in joint session, Congress listens to President Johnson's legislative proposals in his State of the Union address in 1966.

not to receive them and thus the power to refuse recognition to a foreign government.

Sect. 4. The president, vice-president and all civil officers of the United States, shall be removed from office on impeachment for, and conviction of, treason, bribery, or other high crimes and misdemeanors.

See Article I, Sections 2 (p. 137) and 3 (p. 139).

Congressmen are not considered "civil officers." They may be removed from office only by a two-thirds majority in their own house. (See Article I, Section 5, p. 140).

163

Article III

Sect. 1. The judicial power of the United States, shall be vested in one supreme court, and in such inferior courts as the Congress may from time to time ordain and establish. The judges, both of the supreme and inferior courts, shall hold their offices during good behaviour, and shall, at stated times, receive for their services, a compensation, which shall not be diminished during their continuance in office.

The Constitution specifies a supreme court, but Congress has established the entire federal court system below the level of the U.S. Supreme Court and has defined its jurisdiction. "Good behaviour" means that the judge is appointed for life, unless he loses office through the impeachment procedure.

Sect. 2. The judicial power shall extend to all cases, in law and equity, arising under this constitution, the laws of the United States, and treaties made, or which shall be made, under their authority; to all cases affecting ambassadors, other public ministers and consuls; to all cases of admiralty and maritime jurisdiction; to controversies to which the United States shall be a party; to controversies between two or more States, between a state and citizens of another state, between citizens of different States, between citizens of the same state claiming lands under grants of different States, and between a state, or the citizens thereof, and foreign States, citizens or subjects.

The phrase "extend to all cases" means that the federal courts may handle all cases in which an interpretation of the Constitution or some U.S. law or treaty is necessary in order to arrive at a judgment. A person who believes his constitutional rights were violated in a trial in a state court may appeal to the U.S. Supreme Court. Or a person who has been convicted under a state law he believes is unconstitutional may appeal his case to the U.S. Supreme

Federal Court System

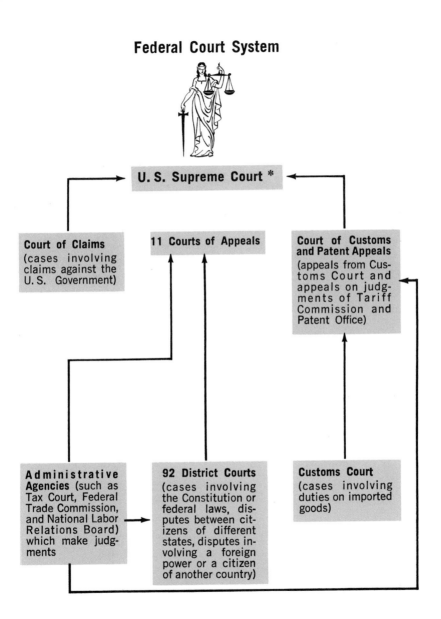

U. S. Supreme Court *

Court of Claims (cases involving claims against the U. S. Government)

11 Courts of Appeals

Court of Customs and Patent Appeals (appeals from Customs Court and appeals on judgments of Tariff Commission and Patent Office)

Administrative Agencies (such as Tax Court, Federal Trade Commission, and National Labor Relations Board) which make judgments

92 District Courts (cases involving the Constitution or federal laws, disputes between citizens of different states, disputes involving a foreign power or a citizen of another country)

Customs Court (cases involving duties on imported goods)

* Appeals may be made from the highest state court, in most states called the Supreme Court, to the U.S. Supreme Court in cases involving federal laws or the U.S. Constitution.

Court. When the Supreme Court decides a case in which the constitutionality of a state or federal law is at stake, it is exercising *judicial review* (see p. 99).

The phrase "ambassadors . . ." means officials of a foreign country. Even though they may be on trial for breaking a state law, they are tried in a federal court. This is because the federal government is responsible for the relations between the U.S. and other countries.

"Admiralty and maritime" cases are those involving ships and shipping.

The phrase "between a state and citizens of another state" has been changed by Amendment 11 (see p. 179).

> In all cases affecting ambassadors, other public ministers and consuls, and those in which a state shall be party, the supreme court shall have original jurisdiction. In all the other cases before mentioned, the supreme court shall have appellate jurisdiction, both as to law and fact, with such exceptions, and under such regulations as the Congress shall make.

The phrase "original jurisdiction" means the power to act as a first court to hear a case. "Appellate jurisdiction" is the power to hear appeals on the verdicts of cases that were heard in a lower court.

> The trial of all crimes, except in cases of impeachment, shall be by jury; and such trial shall be held in the state where the said crimes shall have been committed; but when not committed within any state, the trial shall be at such place or places as the Congress may by law have directed.

See also Amendment 6, p. 177.

> *Sect.* 3. Treason against the United States, shall consist only in levying war against them, or in adhering to their enemies, giving them aid and comfort. No person shall be

convicted of treason unless on the testimony of two witnesses to the same overt act, or on confession in open court.

A person cannot be convicted of treason unless two witnesses testify that they actually saw the treasonable act or unless the accused person confesses in open court.

The Congress shall have power to declare the punishment of treason, but no attainder of treason shall work corruption of blood, or forfeiture except during the life of the person attainted.

Congress can fix the penalty for treason. But a treason conviction cannot "work corruption of blood"; that is, it cannot prevent the convicted person's heirs from collecting what he willed to them.

Article IV

Sect. I. Full faith and credit shall be given in each state to the public acts, records, and judicial proceedings of every

Supreme Court Justices pose for photograph after Fortas (standing, rt.) replaced Goldberg. Chief Justice Warren is seated at center.

UPI

other state. And the Congress may by general laws prescribe the manner in which such acts, records and proceedings shall be proved, and the effect thereof.

A birth certificate, issued in the state where the birth took place, for example, is valid in every other state.

Sect. 2. The citizens of each state shall be entitled to all privileges and immunities of citizens in the several states.

A New Yorker in Arizona enjoys the same rights and privileges as a native Arizonian. Arizona might make certain privileges depend on actual residence in the state, however.

A person charged in any state with treason, felony, or other crime, who shall flee from justice, and be found in another state, shall, on demand of the executive authority of the state from which he fled, be delivered up, to be removed to the state having jurisdiction of the crime.

When a person flees from one state to another to escape arrest, the second state must return him to the first. Yet if the second state chooses not to send him back, there is no legal machinery to force it to do so. But Congress has passed laws making it illegal to flee from state to state to escape prosecution for certain crimes. In such cases, federal officers can seize the fugitive and return him to the federal judicial district where the crime was supposed to have been committed. Then he is turned over to state officials for trial.

[No person held to service or labour in one state, under the laws thereof, escaping into another, shall, in consequence of any law or regulation therein, be discharged from such service or labour, but shall be delivered up on claim of the party to whom such service or labour may be due.]

Amendment 13 canceled this paragraph (see p. 182).

Sect. 3. New states may be admitted by the Congress into this union; but no new state shall be formed or erected within the jurisdiction of any other state; nor any state be formed by the junction of two or more states, or parts of states, without the consent of the legislatures of the states concerned as well as of the Congress.

Each new state admitted to the union is equal to those already members. Its citizens have the same rights and privileges under the Constitution as the citizens of the other states.

The Congress shall have power to dispose of and make all needful rules and regulations respecting the territory or other property belonging to the United States; and nothing in this Constitution shall be so construed as to prejudice any claims of the United States, or of any particular state.

This paragraph gives Congress power to govern new territories added to the U.S. The Supreme Court has ruled that in unincorporated territories — those not considered part of the U.S. — "fundamental" parts of the Constitution, such as the right to freedom of speech, apply. Congress decides whether the remainder of the Constitution applies also.

Sect. 4. The United States shall guarantee to every state in this union a Republican form of government, and shall protect each of them against invasion; and on application of the legislature, or of the executive (when the legislature cannot be convened) against domestic violence.

By a "Republican form of government" the makers of the Constitution probably meant a government operated by elected representatives of the people. When Congress seats a state's representatives, it acknowledges indirectly that the state's government is legal under the Constitution.

Newest states, Hawaii (top) and Alaska, celebrate their admission to the Union. Congress voted in 1958 to admit Alaska, and in 1959, Hawaii. Then President Eisenhower made it official by proclamation.

Article V

The Congress, whenever two-thirds of both houses shall deem it necessary, shall propose amendments to this constitution, or, on the application of the legislatures of two-thirds of the several states, shall call a convention for proposing amendments, which, in either case, shall be valid to all intents and purposes, as part of this constitution, when ratified by the legislatures of three-fourths of the several states, or by conventions in three-fourths thereof, as the one or the other mode of ratification may be proposed by the Congress; Provided, that no amendment which may be made prior to the year one thousand eight hundred and eight shall in any manner affect the first and fourth clauses in the ninth section of the first article; and that no state, without its consent, shall be deprived of its equal suffrage in the senate.

All constitutional amendments so far have been proposed by a two-thirds vote of both houses of Congress. Under the Constitution a national convention called by Congress at the request of two thirds of the state legislatures could also propose an amendment. Proposed amendments must be ratified by three fourths of the state legislatures or by special state conventions in three fourths of the states. Amendment 21 (see p. 190) was ratified by the second method; all the others, by the first.

Article VI

All debts contracted and engagements entered into, before the adoption of this Constitution, shall be as valid against the United States under this Constitution, as under the confederation.

The U.S. under the Constitution made itself responsible for debts contracted by the Congress under the Articles of Confederation.

This constitution, and the laws of the United States which shall be made in pursuance thereof; and all treaties made, or which shall be made, under the authority of the United States, shall be the supreme law of the land; and the judges in every state shall be bound thereby, any thing in the constitution or laws of any state to the contrary notwithstanding.

Led by Speaker Sam Rayburn (1882-1961), members of the House of Representatives swear to support the Constitution at start of 87th session. "Mr. Sam" served longer than any other man as Speaker.

The senators and representatives beforementioned, and the members of the several state legislatures, and all executive and judicial officers, both of the United States and of the several States, shall be bound by oath or affirmation, to support this constitution; but no religious test shall ever be required as a qualification to any office or public trust under the United States.

These two paragraphs establish the supremacy of the Constitution, federal laws, and treaties over state constitutions and state laws in those areas delegated to the federal government by the Constitution. If a state constitution or a state law conflicts with "the supreme law of the land," it is invalid.

A federal official's religion — or lack of it — must never be considered as a test of his qualifications for office.

Article VII

The ratification of the conventions of nine States, shall be sufficient for the establishment of this constitution between the States so ratifying the same.

There were thirteen states when the Constitution was offered as the law of the land. Actually eleven ratified before the Constitution was declared in effect in 1789.

Done in Convention, by the unanimous consent of the States present, the seventeenth day of September, in the year of our Lord one thousand seven hundred and eighty-seven, and of the Independence of the United States of America the twelfth. In witness whereof we have hereunto subscribed our Names.

GEORGE WASHINGTON, *President,*
And **Deputy from VIRGINIA.**

NEW-HAMPSHIRE.
John Langdon,
Nicholas Gilman.

MASSACHUSETTS.
Nathaniel Gorham,
Rufus King.

CONNECTICUT.
William Samuel Johnson,
Roger Sherman.

NEW-YORK.
Alexander Hamilton.

NEW-JERSEY.
William Livingston,
David Brearley,
William Paterson,
Jonathan Dayton.

PENNSYLVANIA.
Benjamin Franklin,
Thomas Mifflin,
Robert Morris,
George Clymer,
Thomas Fitzsimons,
Jared Ingersoll,
James Wilson,
Gouverneur Morris.

DELAWARE.
George Read,
Gunning Bedford, Junior,
John Dickinson,
Richard Bassett,
Jacob Broom.

MARYLAND.
James M'Henry,
Daniel of St. Tho. Jenifer,
Daniel Carrol.

VIRGINIA.
John Blair,
James Madison, Junior.

NORTH-CAROLINA.
William Blount,
Richard Dobbs Spaight,
Hugh Williamson.

SOUTH-CAROLINA.
John Rutledge,
Charles Cotesworth Pinckney,
Charles Pinckney,
Pierce Butler.

GEORGIA.
William Few,
Abraham Baldwin.

Attest, *William Jackson,* SECRETARY.

Amendments

The first ten amendments, called the Bill of Rights, were proposed during the first year of the First Congress — 1789. They were ratified and became part of the Constitution in 1791. The Bill of Rights filled what many considered to be a serious gap in the Constitution. These first ten amendments are often cited as the cornerstone of individual freedom in the United States.

Amendment I

Congress shall make no law respecting an establishment of religion, or prohibiting the free exercise thereof; or abridging the freedom of speech, or of the press; or the right of the people peaceably to assemble, and to petition the Government for a redress of grievances.

The First Amendment says that *Congress* shall not deprive a person of certain freedoms. Amendment 14 says, in effect, that the *states* shall not deprive a person of the same rights. But deciding when one of these freedoms is being breached has always been up to the courts. Thomas Jefferson said that the religion clause set "a wall between church and state." That interpretation was broadened in 1962 when the Supreme Court ruled that

Negro and white citizens exercise their right "peaceably to assemble" and petition the government in this 1963 March on Washington.

religious exercises in public schools were an infringement of religious freedom. In 1964, however, Congress passed a school aid bill which granted financial help to certain activities of parochial schools.

Freedom of speech and of the press are not absolute and unconditional rights. There are laws against slander and libel, for example. And when the exercise of freedom of speech leads to a "clear and present danger" to the community as a whole or to individuals in it, that freedom may be limited. Said Supreme Court Justice Oliver Wendell Holmes, in a colorful illustration, freedom of speech does not give a person the right to shout "Fire!" in a crowded theatre.

Picketing, demonstrating, and the various forms of "sit-ins" are examples of the "right of the people peaceably to assemble." The key word is "peaceably."

Amendment 2

A well regulated Militia, being necessary to the security of a free State, the right of the people to keep and bear Arms, shall not be infringed.

This does not deny the right of states to pass laws against carrying or owning unlicensed firearms, especially "concealed weapons." It does protect the right to bear arms for lawful purposes.

Amendment 3

No Soldier shall, in time of peace be quartered in any house, without the consent of the Owner, nor in time of war, but in a manner to be prescribed by law.

In colonial days, British soldiers were lodged in private homes. This amendment was written to prevent a recurrence of that unhappy experience.

Amendment 4

The right of the people to be secure in their persons, houses, papers, and effects, against unreasonable searches and seizures, shall not be violated, and no Warrants shall issue, but upon probable cause, supported by Oath or affirmation, and particularly describing the place to be searched, and the persons or things to be seized.

This amendment prevents federal officials from making unlawful searches. Under Amendment 14, state and local officers are also forbidden to engage in "unreasonable searches and seizures" (see p. 183). What "unreasonable" means is left to the courts to define.

Amendment 5

No person shall be held to answer for a capital, or otherwise infamous crime, unless on a presentment or indictment of a Grand Jury, except in cases arising in the land or naval forces, or in the Militia, when in actual service in time of War or public danger; nor shall any person be subject for the same offence to be twice put in jeopardy of life or limb; nor shall be compelled in any criminal case to be a witness against himself, nor be deprived of life, liberty, or property, without due process of law; nor shall private property be taken for public use, without just compensation.

A "capital, or otherwise infamous crime" is murder or other crime almost as serious. A "presentment or indictment of a Grand Jury" is an accusation by a jury of not more than twenty-three members. The votes of twelve of them are enough to make the accusation stick and bring the accused to trial.

"Twice put in jeopardy" means that a person may not be tried again, once acquitted of a crime. "Nor . . . compelled . . . to be a witness against himself" means that a person can refuse to answer any question when his answer

The jury at a murder trial in California was photographed before court was called to order to comply with state law banning cameras.

may subject him to criminal prosecution. The "due process" clause here applies only to federal laws and court procedures. The same phrase is repeated in Amendment 14 where it applies to state laws and state courts (see p. 183).

Amendment 6

In all criminal prosecutions, the accused shall enjoy the right to a speedy and public trial, by an impartial jury of the State and district wherein the crime shall have been committed, which district shall have been previously ascertained by law, and to be informed of the nature and cause of the accusation; to be confronted with the witnesses against him; to have compulsory process for obtaining witnesses in his favor, and to have the Assistance of Counsel for his defence.

The accused, not the press, is entitled to a public trial. News photographers and television cameramen are usually barred from otherwise "public" trials to prevent disruptions in the proceedings. An "impartial jury" means, among other considerations, one from which jurors of the same race, nationality, or religion as the accused are not barred. Sometimes the accused and his lawyer do not believe that an "impartial jury" can be chosen in the "district wherein the crime shall have been committed." The people in the district may have been unduly aroused and, perhaps, prejudiced by news accounts of the crime. Then the defense can ask for a "change of venue" — a trial in another district, where an "impartial" jury may be found.

Witnesses against the accused must testify in open court, and the defense attorney must be permitted to question ("cross-examine") them. "Assistance of Counsel" means that the court must provide a lawyer for the accused if he is unable to pay for one himself.

Amendment 7

In Suits at common law, where the value in controversy shall exceed twenty dollars, the right of trial by jury shall be preserved, and no fact tried by a jury, shall be otherwise re-examined in any Court of the United States, than according to the rules of the common law.

In some civil cases a jury may be dispensed with if the two parties agree to let the judge make the decision and the judge consents to do so.

Amendment 8

Excessive bail shall not be required, nor excessive fines imposed, nor cruel and unusual punishments inflicted.

"Bail" is a sum of money the accused deposits with the court. He may then go free until his trial. The purpose is to free the accused to prepare for his trial. If he runs away, he "forfeits the bail" — the federal or state government keeps the bail money. The accused, however, still is liable to trial.

Amendment 9

The enumeration in the Constitution, of certain rights, shall not be construed to deny or disparage others retained by the people.

This amendment states that the Constitution lists some, but not all, of the rights of the people. One of those not listed, according to the Supreme Court, is the right to engage in political activity.

Amendment 10

The powers not delegated to the United States by the Constitution, nor prohibited by it to the States, are reserved to the States respectively, or to the people.

This amendment does not set a limit on federal powers. Within those areas delegated to it by the Constitution, the federal government has full power — even though it may interfere in the states. For example, public schools are usually considered the responsibility of the states. But the federal government has passed school-aid bills under its implied powers, thus moving into an area once thought to belong only to the states.

Reserved power — all power in areas not specifically delegated to the federal government — belongs to the states or the people.

Amendment 11

The Judicial power of the United States shall not be construed to extend to any suit in law or equity, commenced or prosecuted against one of the United States by Citizens of another State, or by Citizens or Subjects of any Foreign State.

This amendment was proposed in 1794, adopted 1798. A citizen of one state cannot sue the government of another state in a federal court as Article III, Section 2, (see p. 164) once said he could.

Amendment 12

The Electors shall meet in their respective states, and vote by ballot for President, and Vice-President, one of whom, at

How Federal Government and States Divide Powers

Our national Constitution provides that certain government powers be

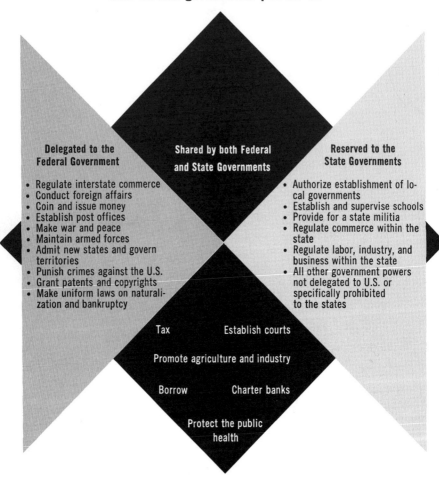

Delegated to the Federal Government

- Regulate interstate commerce
- Conduct foreign affairs
- Coin and issue money
- Establish post offices
- Make war and peace
- Maintain armed forces
- Admit new states and govern territories
- Punish crimes against the U.S.
- Grant patents and copyrights
- Make uniform laws on naturalization and bankruptcy

Shared by both Federal and State Governments

Tax   Establish courts

Promote agriculture and industry

Borrow   Charter banks

Protect the public health

Reserved to the State Governments

- Authorize establishment of local governments
- Establish and supervise schools
- Provide for a state militia
- Regulate commerce within the state
- Regulate labor, industry, and business within the state
- All other government powers not delegated to U.S. or specifically prohibited to the states

PROHIBITED POWERS

The personal rights of people of the United States, as listed in the Bill of Rights (first ten Amendments to the Constitution) cannot be reduced or destroyed by the federal or the state governments.

least, shall not be an inhabitant of the same state with themselves; they shall name in their ballots the person voted for as President and in distinct ballots the person voted for as Vice-President, and they shall make distinct lists of all persons voted for as President, and of all persons voted for as Vice-President, and of the number of votes for each, which lists they shall sign and certify, and transmit sealed to the seat of the government of the United States, directed to the President of the Senate;—The President of the Senate shall, in the presence of the Senate and House of Representatives, open all the certificates and the votes shall then be counted;—The person having the greatest number of votes for President, shall be the President, if such number be a majority of the whole number of Electors appointed; and if no person have such majority, then from the persons having the highest numbers not exceeding three on the list of those voted for as President, the House of Representatives shall choose immediately, by ballot, the President. But in choosing the President, the votes shall be taken by states, the representation from each state having one vote; a quorum for this purpose shall consist of a member or members from two-thirds of the states, and a majority of all the states shall be necessary to a choice. [And if the House of Representatives shall not choose a President whenever the right of choice shall devolve upon them, before the fourth day of March next following, then the Vice-President shall act as President, as in the case of the death or other constitutional disability of the President.]— The person having the greatest number of votes as Vice-President, shall be the Vice-President, if such number be a majority of the whole number of Electors appointed, and if no person have a majority, then from the two highest numbers on the list, the Senate shall choose the Vice-President; a quorum for the purpose shall consist of two-thirds of the whole number of Senators, and a majority of the whole number shall be necessary to a choice. But no person constitutionally ineligible to the office of President shall be eligible to that of Vice-President of the United States.

This amendment was proposed in 1803, adopted 1804. It was made necessary by the rise of political parties and replaces part of Article II, Section 1 (see p. 156). The part of this amendment enclosed in brackets has been replaced by Amendment 20, Section 3 (see p. 188). Note also Amendment 23 (see p. 191). Since the adoption of Amendment 12, the House of Representatives has been called upon to choose the President only once. In 1824 Andrew Jackson, John Quincy Adams, and William H. Crawford won the most electoral votes, but none had a majority. The House, voting by states, elected Adams. The Senate has been called upon only once to elect the Vice-President — in 1837, when it chose Richard M. Johnson over Francis Granger.

The winning candidate in each state receives all that state's electoral votes (see p. 156). A few times in the past a Presidential candidate has received the greater nationwide popular vote but the lesser state-by-state electoral vote, and so lost the election.

Amendment 13

Section 1. Neither slavery nor involuntary servitude, except as a punishment for crime whereof the party shall have been duly convicted, shall exist within the United States, or any place subject to their jurisdiction.

Section 2. Congress shall have power to enforce this article by appropriate legislation.

This amendment was proposed in 1865, adopted the same year. It banned slavery in any and all of the United States. Importing of slaves had been banned in 1809 under Article I, Section 9. In addition, many states had banned slavery before this amendment was proposed.

Amendment 14

Section 1. All persons born or naturalized in the United States, and subject to the jurisdiction thereof, are citizens of the United States and of the State wherein they reside. No State shall make or enforce any law which shall abridge the privileges or immunities of citizens of the United States; nor shall any State deprive any person of life, liberty, or property, without due process of law; nor deny to any person within its jurisdiction the equal protection of the laws.

Section 2. Representatives shall be apportioned among the several States according to their respective numbers, counting the whole number of persons in each State, excluding Indians not taxed. But when the right to vote at any election for the choice of electors for President and Vice President of the United States, Representatives in Congress, the Executive and Judicial officers of a State, or the members of the Legislature thereof, is denied to any of the male inhabitants of such State, being twenty-one years of age, and citizens of the United States, or in any way abridged, except for participation in rebellion, or other crime, the basis of representation therein shall be reduced in the proportion which the number of such male citizens shall bear to the whole number of male citizens twenty-one years of age in such State.

Section 3. No person shall be a Senator or Representative in Congress, or elector of President and Vice President, or hold any office, civil or military, under the United States, or under any State, who, having previously taken an oath, as a member of Congress, or as an officer of the United States, or as a member of any State legislature, or as an executive or judicial officer of any State, to support the Constitution of the United States, shall have engaged in insurrection or rebellion against the same, or given aid or comfort to the enemies thereof. But Congress may by a vote of two-thirds of each House, remove such disability.

Many schools began to integrate after 1954 when the Supreme Court ruled that segregation denied "equal protection of the laws."

Section 4. The validity of the public debt of the United States, authorized by law, including debts incurred for payment of pensions and bounties for services in suppressing insurrection or rebellion, shall not be questioned. But neither the United States nor any State shall assume or pay any debt or obligation incurred in aid of insurrection or rebellion against the United States, or any claim for the loss or emancipation of any slave; but all such debts, obligations and claims shall be held illegal and void.

Section 5. The Congress shall have power to enforce, by appropriate legislation, the provisions of this article.

This amendment was proposed in 1866, adopted 1868. It makes citizens of *all* persons — no matter what their race or original nationality — who are either born in the U.S. or are naturalized. And it says that the states cannot "abridge" — cut short or destroy — the "privileges and immunities" guaranteed to all U.S. citizens by the Constitution.

184

Amendment 5 says that the federal government cannot deprive a person of life, liberty, or property, without "due process of law" (see p. 177). Amendment 14 forbids the states to do so as well. Through Supreme Court interpretation, "liberty" has come to include many of the freedoms listed in the Bill of Rights.

The U.S. Supreme Court based its 1954 decision ending school segregation on the "equal protection of the laws" phrase. Its 1964 decision, ruling that state legislative districts were to be reapportioned on the basis of population, was also based partly on this phrase (see p. 137), as were various civil rights laws.

Section 2 of this amendment replaces a part of Article I, Section 2 (see p. 136).

Section 3 was intended to prevent those who had led the southern states in the Civil War from holding political office. In 1898 Congress did remove the "disability." Today this clause is of historical interest only.

Section 4 relieved the U.S. government of debts contracted during the Civil War by the Confederacy.

As the deadline for paying federal income tax approaches, taxpayers swarm into the local office of the Internal Revenue Service.

Amendment 15

Section 1. The right of citizens of the United States to vote shall not be denied or abridged by the United States or by any State on account of race, color, or previous condition of servitude.

Section 2. The Congress shall have power to enforce this article by appropriate legislation.

This amendment was proposed in 1869, adopted 1870. Some states continued to find ways to keep Negroes from voting, however, and the Voting Rights Act of 1965 was passed to help implement this amendment.

Amendment 16

The Congress shall have power to lay and collect taxes on incomes, from whatever source derived, without apportionment among the several States, and without regard to any census or enumeration.

This amendment was proposed in 1909, adopted 1913. It is the basis for all federal income tax legislation (see Article 1, Section 9, p. 152).

Amendment 17

The Senate of the United States shall be composed of two Senators from each State, elected by the people thereof, for six years; and each Senator shall have one vote. The electors in each State shall have the qualifications requisite for electors of the most numerous branch of the State legislatures.

When vacancies happen in the representation of any State in the Senate, the executive authority of such State shall issue writs of election to fill such vacancies: *Provided,* That the legislature of any State may empower the executive thereof to make temporary appointments until the people fill the vacancies by election as the legislature may direct.

This amendment shall not be so construed as to affect the election or term of any Senator chosen before it becomes valid as part of the Constitution.

This amendment was proposed in 1912, adopted 1913. It replaces the phrase in Article I, Section 3, that authorizes state legislatures to choose U.S. Senators (see p. 137). Voters in the states now elect the Senators from their states.

Amendment 18

[Section 1. After one year from the ratification of this article the manufacture, sale, or transportation of intoxicating liquors within, the importation thereof into, or the exportation thereof from the United States and all territory subject to the jurisdiction thereof for beverage purposes is hereby prohibited.

[Sec. 2. The Congress and the several States shall have concurrent power to enforce this article by appropriate legislation.

[Sec. 3. This article shall be inoperative unless it shall have been ratified as an amendment to the Constitution by the legislatures of the several States, as provided in the Constitution, within seven years from the date of the submission hereof to the States by the Congress.]

This amendment was proposed in 1917, adopted 1919. Called by some the "Noble Experiment," Prohibition was repealed in 1933 by Amendment 21 (see p. 190).

Amendment 19

The right of citizens of the United States to vote shall not be denied or abridged by the United States or by any State on account of sex.

Congress shall have power to enforce this article by appropriate legislation.

Suffragettes campaigned for seventy years before finally securing passage of the 19th Amendment. Here they parade in New York.

This amendment was proposed in 1919, adopted 1920. Some states had already given women the same voting rights as men. Amendment 19 made woman suffrage nationwide.

Amendment 20

Section 1. The terms of the President and Vice President shall end at noon on the 20th day of January, and the terms of Senators and Representatives at noon on the 3d day of January, of the years in which such terms would have ended if this article had not been ratified; and the terms of their successors shall then begin.

Sec. 2. The Congress shall assemble at least once in every year, and such meeting shall begin at noon on the 3d day of January, unless they shall by law appoint a different day.

Sec. 3. If, at the time fixed for the beginning of the term of the President, the President elect shall have died, the Vice President elect shall become President. If a President shall not have been chosen before the time fixed for the beginning of his term, or if the President elect shall have failed to qualify, then the Vice President elect shall act as President until a President shall have qualified; and the Congress may by law provide for the case wherein neither a President elect nor a Vice President elect shall have qualified, declaring who shall then act as President, or the manner in which one who is to act shall be selected, and such person shall act accordingly until a President or Vice President shall have qualified.

Sec. 4. The Congress may by law provide for the case of the death of any of the persons from whom the House of Representatives may choose a President whenever the right of choice shall have devolved upon them, and for the case of the death of any of the persons from whom the Senate may choose a Vice President whenever the right of choice shall have devolved upon them.

Sec. 5. Sections 1 and 2 shall take effect on the 15th day of October following the ratification of this article.

Sec. 6. This article shall be inoperative unless it shall have been ratified as an amendment to the Constitution by the legislatures of three-fourths of the several States within seven years from the date of its submission.

This amendment was proposed in 1932, adopted 1933. Before the amendment was passed, a defeated President and Vice-President continued in office from the November election until the following March 4. Defeated Congressmen served until the session ended in March and newly elected Congressmen did not take their seats until Congress reconvened as late as December, thirteen months after they were elected. Defeated Congressmen, still serving, were called "lame ducks."

Section 2 replaces a paragraph in Article 1, Section 4 (see p. 140).

Amendment 21

Section 1. The eighteenth article of amendment to the Constitution of the United States is hereby repealed.

Sec. 2. The transportation or importation into any State, Territory, or possession of the United States for delivery or use therein of intoxicating liquors, in violation of the laws thereof, is hereby prohibited.

Sec. 3. This article shall be inoperative unless it shall have been ratified as an amendment to the Constitution by conventions in the several States, as provided in the Constitution, within seven years from the date of the submission hereof to the States by the Congress.

This amendment was proposed in 1933, adopted the same year. It repeals Amendment 18 (see p. 187).

Despite efforts by government agents (shown here dumping beer) to enforce the 18th Amendment, Prohibition failed and was repealed.

Amendment 22

Section 1. No person shall be elected to the office of the President more than twice, and no person who has held the office of President, or acted as President, for more than two years of a term to which some other person was elected President shall be elected to the office of the President more than once. But this Article shall not apply to any person holding the office of President when this Article was proposed by the Congress, and shall not prevent any person who may be holding the office of President, or acting as President, during the term within which this Article becomes operative from holding the office of President or acting as President during the remainder of such term.

Sec. 2. This article shall be inoperative unless it shall have been ratified as an amendment to the Constitution by the legislatures of three-fourths of the several States within seven years from the date of its submission to the States by the Congress.

This amendment was proposed in 1947, adopted 1951. If a Vice-President succeeds to the Presidency with less than two years of the former, or late, President's term remaining, as did Lyndon B. Johnson, he may be elected for two more terms. If he succeeds to the Presidency with more than two years to serve, he may be elected for only one more term. In any case, a President may serve a maximum of ten years. The amendment was proposed when Harry S. Truman was President (1945-1953), but it did not apply to him. He was entitled to run for another term, but he did not choose to.

Amendment 23

Section 1. The District constituting the seat of Government of the United States shall appoint in such manner as the Congress may direct:

A number of electors of President and Vice President equal to the whole number of Senators and Representatives in Congress to which the District would be entitled if it were a State, but in no event more than the least populous State; they shall be in addition to those appointed by the States, but they shall be considered, for the purposes of the election of President and Vice President, to be electors appointed by a State; and they shall meet in the District and perform such duties as provided by the twelfth article of amendment.

Section 2. The Congress shall have power to enforce this article by appropriate legislation.

This amendment was proposed in 1960, adopted 1961. It permits qualified residents of the District of Columbia to vote for President and Vice-President.

Amendment 24

Section 1. The right of citizens of the United States to vote in any primary or other election for President or Vice President, for electors for President or Vice President, or for Senator or Representative in Congress, shall not be denied or abridged by the United States or any State by reason of failure to pay any poll tax or other tax.

Section 2. The Congress shall have power to enforce this article by appropriate legislation.

This amendment was proposed in 1962, adopted 1964. It outlawed the poll tax as a requirement for voting in federal elections. At the time the amendment was adopted, five states were imposing such poll taxes. The 1965 Voting Rights Act opened the way for lawsuits challenging poll taxes in state or local elections.

Amendment 25 (proposed)

Section 1. In case of the removal of the President from office or his death or resignation, the Vice President shall become President.

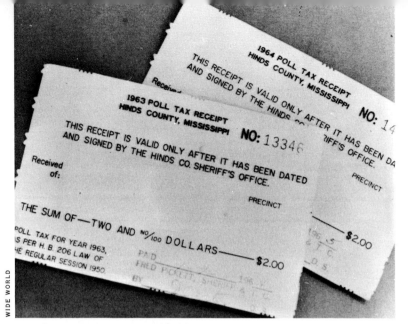

Poll taxes were once used to discourage Negroes from voting. Proof of payment may no longer be required to vote in federal elections.

Section 2. Whenever there is a vacancy in the office of the Vice President, the President shall nominate a Vice President who shall take the office upon confirmation by a majority vote of both houses of Congress.

Section 3. Whenever the President transmits to the President pro tempore of the Senate and the Speaker of the House of Representatives his written declaration that he is unable to discharge the powers and duties of his office, and until he transmits to them a written declaration to the contrary, such powers and duties shall be discharged by the Vice President as Acting President.

Section 4. Whenever the Vice President and a majority of either the principal officers of the executive departments or of such other body as Congress may by law provide, transmit to the President pro tempore of the Senate and the Speaker of the House of Representatives their written declaration that the President is unable to discharge the powers and duties of his office, the Vice President shall immediately assume the powers and duties of the office as Acting President.

Thereafter, when the President transmits to the President pro tempore of the Senate and the Speaker of the House of Representatives his written declaration that no inability exists, he shall resume the powers and duties of his office unless the Vice President and a majority of either the principal officers of the executive department or of such other body as Congress may by law provide, transmit within four days to the President pro tempore of the Senate and the Speaker of the House of Representatives their written declaration that the President is unable to discharge the powers and duties of his office. Thereupon Congress shall decide the issue, assembling within 48 hours for that purpose if not in session. If the Congress, within 21 days after receipt of the latter written declaration, or, if Congress is not in session, within 21 days after Congress is required to assemble, determines by two-thirds vote of both houses that the President is unable to discharge the powers and duties of his office, the Vice President shall continue to discharge the same as Acting President; otherwise, the President shall resume the powers and duties of his office.

This amendment was proposed in 1965. It is intended to clear up the ambiguities in Article II, Section 1, the paragraph beginning "In case of the removal of the president from office . . ." (see p. 158). It sets up a procedure for determining when a President is unable to fulfill his duties so that the Vice-President may take over. In the past some Presidents have remained in office while seriously ill. President Wilson, for example, suffered a stroke and was bedridden for eighteen months.

This amendment would also make certain that the United States is not without a Vice-President for long periods of time as it was after President Kennedy was assassinated and Vice-President Johnson became President.

Index

INDEX

INDEX